*This book is dedicated to the women who have partici-
pated in the Contemporary Woman Programs in Calgary,
Alberta. We are grateful to them for sharing their life experiences so intimately with us and for teaching us so much.*

A Woman's Choice

A Guide to Decision Making

Lorna P. Cammaert · Carolyn C. Larsen

Research Press Company
2612 North Mattis Avenue
Champaign, Illinois 61820

Contents

Exercises

Acknowledgments

Our book is about a process of decision making. We discovered writing a book is itself a fascinating process.

We also found that our authorship was truly a mutual activity, so much so that what each of us originally wrote is no longer distinguishable. Since our ideas, time, and effort have been melded so completely, we consider ourselves equal authors. Someone's name had to be mentioned first, however, so we flipped a coin to make that decision!

In developing the process described in the book, we have been influenced and helped by the professional literature, conferences, workshops, and sharing by colleagues. Whenever possible we have acknowledged the person responsible for an idea or exercise, but if we have inadvertently omitted anyone, please accept our thanks.

Many people have been instrumental in the evaluation of our joint book-writing process. While we will not acknowledge all by name, we are grateful to each one. A few people do need special recognition.

We have already noted our gratitude to Contemporary Woman participants in Calgary, Alberta, by dedicating this book to them. We value their sharing and their allowing us to use their lives as examples in helping others. This is especially true of "Barbara" who deserves special thanks for her extensive self-disclosure.

Throughout the development of the Contemporary Woman Programs, Betty Garbutt has been an inspiration to us. Her unflagging support, creative administration, and caring for the women in the programs have been vital to us and are greatly appreciated.

Also we owe a great deal to the staff of all the Contemporary Woman Programs, a group which has grown large and very special over the years. These competent women have contributed knowledge, innovation, and a warm responsiveness to our developing ideas.

Several people read various drafts of this book and made valuable suggestions. Although we are ultimately responsible for the content, their efforts helped us smooth out a lot of wrinkles. We are grateful to Joan North, Zana Niblack, Mason Niblack, Marilyn Cole, Lana Clark, and Merril McEvoy-Halston for the time and careful thought they gave in their reactions. Ann Wendel and Ann Music Streetman of Research Press were supportive readers and critics whose help was invaluable.

A number of people in several countries have typed various versions of this book. We are indebted to them for their meticulous care, interest, and dedication. We single out Nancy Norman who has been persistently exacting and understanding in her work with us.

We acknowledge the encouragement of our colleagues at Student Counselling Services, University of Calgary. They have maintained the stimulating and supportive atmosphere in which books such as this are nourished.

To our families, Lee, Kris, Keo, and Kirk Handy and Don, Eric, and Dirk Larsen who have patiently waited, enthusiastically anticipated, and consistently provided support, we say thanks.

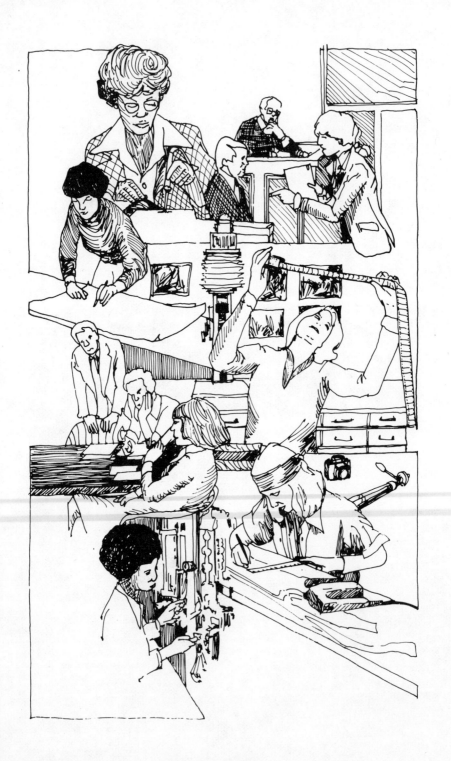

One
Introduction

THE CHANGING ROLES OF WOMEN

This book is the result of our acute awareness of the changing needs of modern women. You as women have increasing options and opportunities for how you can live your lives—you are re-examining and redefining the variety of personal, social, and sexual roles open to you. However, deciding among these options is an awesome task and one for which few women are adequately prepared.

Women of all ages and economic means are taking a look at their current lives and their futures with a new feeling that they can more directly choose how they will express themselves as individuals. This book is written to help you look at your own lifestyle and make decisions about your personal future direction.

This book is also the outgrowth of several programs for women called *Contemporary Woman: Options and Opportunities* which we were instrumental in developing. Four sponsoring and coordinating agencies have been involved in the Contemporary Woman programs: Division of Continuing Education, Calgary Board of Education; Faculty of Continuing Education, and Student Counselling Services, The University of Calgary; and Alberta Advanced Education and Manpower. The program was first developed for married, middle-class women who could afford to pay a small fee. With some modifications the program was expanded, and groups were offered for women on social assistance, mostly single parents. The situations and problems with which the women have to deal are as varied as the persons involved in the groups. However, there appear to be more similarities than differences among them as they discuss their roles, situations, and problems. The Contemporary Woman programs help women in various economic positions to discover their goals, skills, aptitudes, and interests. Also information is provided about opportunities for women in educational, vocational, volunteer, creative, leisure, and domestic activities. Using the personal information and the community resources, the women learn how to make good decisions and how to make a short-term and a long-term life plan for themselves. Making a decision that is uniquely suitable for the individual is stressed. Programs similar to these have sprung up all over North America to help meet the challenge of today's restless women.

This restlessness in women has been partly brought about by changes in society and technology. These changes have made it possible for women to broaden the scope of their choices. The place of woman in society in her many roles—student, daughter, worker, wife, mother, widow, grandmother—has been changing and expanding rapidly over the last 25 years, often with stunning speed. Individually women are viewing themselves and learning to view women in general as people who can make choices about their lives. They are participating more actively in society through their work and in politics, and they are becoming more visible in places of influence.

Even if you are not a feminist or do not support the Women's Movement, you are probably aware of and affected by the efforts to examine and change laws and attitudes to allow equal opportunities for women in work, education, and indeed in every arena of living. As more and more women consider and successfully try new combinations of roles, some of the ideas about the status and equality of women that may have seemed radical a few years ago are now beginning to seem more reasonable and right.

The traditional pattern of completing an education, working, marrying, raising a family, and putting the roles of wife and mother first in life is still workable and important. However, it is no longer the only choice or sequence that women see for themselves. Living through other people and deriving identity mainly because of relationships to others is no longer enough for many women. "There must be something more to life" is commonly heard from today's women who find living mainly through others unfulfilling.

Many women have been thrust out of the traditional pattern through divorce. Statistics now often quoted show 2 out of every 4 marriages ending in divorce.[1] Women are being deserted, and women are also deserting their families and deciding that divorce is a good or the only alternative for them. Even if a woman decides on a traditional life pattern, circumstances may alter the decision dramatically, often causing sudden and disruptive changes in her life. She must learn to cope with her seesawing feelings of fear, relief, joy, and sorrow as she carries out her new lifestyle. Often there appear to be few or no attractive options available to her, but the circumstances may help her expand her horizons to discover that there are more options and opportunities.

Women from minorities and low socioeconomic positions often are forced into a nontraditional family pattern so that they can support themselves and their children. The traditional pattern seems luxurious since working is a life necessity for them. However, it is difficult for many women to find work that pays enough to provide a decent life. The lack of adequate day and night child care and the individual's restricted educational background and work experience are limiting factors. For some of these women a life plan is important to ensure that they do not get trapped in a low-paying, low-status, low-promotion job.

Other women have been trying out alternative patterns which have been successful for them: having both a career and a family, having marriage and a career with no children, remaining single and having a career as a central life focus, living in a corporate marriage or commune, or living sequentially with different people. Within each of these alternatives there are many variations.

THE NEED FOR DECISION MAKING

To move from the traditional plan for a woman's life to a new one forces a person to make decisions about herself. Such decisions are not easy, especially since most women have not been taught or expected to make them. Women usually do not make decisions as independent people but almost always in relation to other people: first parents, then boyfriends, husbands, bosses, children, friends, and grandchildren. Too often women do not consciously make decisions about their lives but drift into behavior patterns and lifestyles by default. It seems natural to drift into decisions while serving the needs of husband, mate, children, etc., or while following the example of others. Since this "drifting" (instead of making rational decisions) usually results in doing what society expects, women are rewarded for doing the "right" thing. The pressures to take on a traditional role of wife and mother are strong and immediate. Most women do marry and have children. However, many become confused when they end up feeling depressed, bored, irritable, and frustrated, despite having done the "right" thing.

With gradually changing attitudes toward women's roles, there is now a conflicting pressure on them. Some women are truly contented and fulfilled in the homemaker role. However, the role is devalued. The new message is that you *should* do something more than be wife and mother if you really want to reach your potential as a person. These double messages (for example, to be fulfilled you must marry and have children, but to be a homemaker is not enough) produce yet another bind for women. This double bind makes it all the more necessary for each woman to make her own decision, according to her own situation and network of relationships, obligations, and commitments.

This book assumes that people can control what happens to them. *You are not preprogrammed to an inevitable outcome.* There are many choice points when you need to look at the consequences of selecting different alternatives. Some choice points may seem small but have significant long-term effects and therefore need careful consideration. Others concern larger decisions such as: if and whom to marry; what type of career to choose; where to live; how many, if any, children to have; whether to divorce. Usually the latter decisions have more obvious possible outcomes than the smaller choice points, but both have consequences.

The goal of this book is to assist you as a woman to examine possible alternatives to reach a realistic decision about yourself and your lifestyle. It is also to help you begin to put that decision into practice. The focus is on decision making that allows you to create and implement a situation in which you feel more fulfilled and satisfied. In this decision making the focus is on you as the central individual. While you continue to care about your social and family responsibilities, you will look at what you want and can do for *yourself*. Each decision is necessarily unique to best fit you and your personal situation, leading to positive consequences for you and for others important to you. The process described in the book is one of self-exploration, decision making, and action.

THE PROCESS AND THE BOOK

Time and Effort Involved

Making a major decision about the direction of your life is a process rather than an end-state. The process is an on-going one which takes time and hard work. It will take time to read the book, to complete the exercises, and to mull over your new learnings. Some of the material may not seem to fit together well until you have been able to think about it over a week or two. Women who previewed the book found they were often interrupted by phone calls, maintenance tasks, children, family demands, etc. They found the interruptions frustrating; they were eager to return to the book. However, it may be necessary to accept the fact that you will be interrupted and that the whole process takes time. Plan on several weeks, at least, to work through the book.

Hard work is necessary to complete the exercises and really think about your answers. Some exercises may reach into areas you have not considered for a long time. Others may involve areas you have been avoiding. Even so, it is important to consider and to work at dealing with each area so that you can make a sound, satisfying decision. This process of working through a critical decision requires careful reflection and solid information.

One woman who previewed the book suggested that a reader approach the contents in three stages: (1) Scan through the book to get an overview of the organization and main ideas; (2) go back through the book carefully, completing the exercises and thinking through the ideas; and (3) review the whole book again to see the pattern and connection of thoughts and your own responses to the exercises. This seems like an effective way to use it.

Sometimes you may ask whether it is worth all the time you are spending on the book, especially the exercises. The women in our groups have found the benefits far outweigh the investment of time and effort. Sometimes you may feel excited or threatened, or questioning, or you may say to yourself, "It *is* worth it!" At the end you will be in a better position to decide a plan for your future. As an added bonus, you will have a set of tools for making decisions in a well-considered rational way.

Once you have reached your decision, it is important to remain open to new experiences and information. This is also a part of the process. The new experiences and information need to be carefully weighed. They may cause you to reconsider your major decision, which may result in some minor, or even major, revision. However, having consciously considered and decided upon the major thrust of your life will help you in making on-going decisions and increase your personal satisfaction.

The process and techniques used here are soundly based in the theory and research of learning psychology. Hundreds of women who have worked with us, individually and in groups, have found the exercises and process helpful.

Individual or Counseling Use

This book is intended for you if you want to examine your personal life and future. We hope to reach those of you who are without the facilities or resources, and those who want some direction as to where and how to start this self-learning project.

All of you, whatever your age, socioeconomic position or cultural background, can benefit from following the decision-making process outlined in the book.

This book is also intended for counselors who work with women. It can be used as a resource for ideas to incorporate into counseling sessions or as homework reading and assignments for clients who can work through the exercises on their own and consolidate their thoughts for future sessions. Hopefully, the ideas will sensitize people who are in a counseling role with girls and women to the complexity of the decision-making process females face in our modern society.

Two
Where Do I Start?

The changes in society and in your own life may have brought you to the point of saying, "I want to do *something, but* . . . ." Various explanations often follow the "but," such as "but I don't know what to do," "but I still have small children," "but who would ever see me as valuable?" "but no one wants someone like me," "but my husband seems to want me at home."

The purpose of this book is to help you answer the questions you have about doing something different, to help you overcome the "buts," and to aid you in developing the confidence to try out alternatives which look as if they are what you want. The major emphasis is to help you find something challenging and interesting that will lead to more fulfillment and feelings of adequacy for having met the challenge.

As you go through the book, you will be asked to consider various aspects of yourself and your particular situation. This is because there are no easy general answers and you must reach your own unique solution. What works for your neighbor or your best friend may or may not be the best alternative for you. The book gives you no "answers." Rather, it provides a guide for your own decision making.

You will be given a set of tools to assist you in assessing your personal background; your assets—everyone has some—and your liabilities—everyone usually has these, too. Then you will be given the opportunity to define your present situation and its advantages and disadvantages. Ideas will be discussed for overcoming some of the most common disadvantages which can quickly become obstacles. At this point the pros and cons connected with your changing will also be highlighted. Part of this involves looking outward to your community and the resources, limitations, and pressures which it provides.

After doing this survey of your assets and limitations, you will be able to consider the question, "Where do I want to go?" A structured way to consider the many possibilities involved in answering this question is provided. Finally, an action program is given for you to follow. It should help you reach whatever goal or goals you have set for yourself.

As you go through the steps that are outlined, keep the following ideas in mind.

1. Remain open to new information and new ideas. Brainstorm; let your imagination roam; allow yourself some fantasies. Do not reject an idea as being "silly," "worthless," or "not me." Remember that you are exploring and that you are gathering *all* information before paring away the impossibles or putting limits on what you will consider.

2. Be honest with yourself. Consider both the negatives and the positives. Most people can think of lots of negative points, but try to leave your modesty behind and focus on your personal positives, too.

3. Put yourself first for a short time each day so that you can complete the program outlined in this book. Most women are used to putting everyone and everything else ahead of themselves. Try to alter this slightly by giving yourself one-half hour per day that is just for you—no interruptions or family demands.

In reading this book and completing the exercises, you will be trying to decide whether to change and what to change. Changing is usually more frightening than staying where you are because it is new and contains elements of risk. Change may also be difficult and seem overwhelming. During the process there may be a period when the usual props or supports you depend upon shift or even disappear for a time. However, change can be exciting, providing growth as well as producing feelings of fulfillment, happiness, and contentment from knowing that you are using your abilities and talents.

Many women report that lack of self-confidence is a block to change. Regardless of employment, marital status, motherhood, age, economic means, education, or skills, there is a persistent feeling of self-doubt. There is a fear of changing, risking a move in a new direction, or trying a new behavior. Perhaps this is your problem, too. Although others may regard you as competent, you may feel you are not competent and never could be. Although there are many degrees of this lack of confidence, the problem does almost paralyze many women, keeping them from acting as fully as they might.

A poor but common way of handling this problem is to set low expectations for yourself so that you do not risk much. *A better method is to develop more feelings of self-confidence through a realistic survey and evaluation of your skills and potential and through encouragement from yourself and others about your plans and achievements.* This book is designed to

help build your self-confidence as you follow the steps it outlines. You may also wish to share the book with a friend so that
you can support each other. Sharing honest support and encouragement can help you both. The pathways of change have ups
and downs, but the places you reach are almost always better
than the place where you started.

DECISION MAKING

You have been making decisions about many different
things for a number of years. As a girl: "Shall I buy the gum-
drops or the licorice?" "Shall I wear the red dress or the plaid
skirt and blouse?" As a young woman: "Shall I finish school or
get married?" "Shall I go to secretarial school or college?"
"Should I get married or stay single?" "Should I have a child? If
so, when?" As a mature woman: "Where will I live?" "Is it
more important for me to have a washing machine or a dryer
first?" "Shall I make hamburgers or meat loaf for supper?"

Some decisions are small and relatively unimportant, whereas others are important and have far-reaching consequences. You may have made decisions by yourself, but to reach some important ones, you may have talked to other people and considered the advantages and disadvantages carefully. At other times the whole weight of the decision may have been overwhelming, so you just threw your hands up in the air, flipped a coin, and went with heads or tails.

•▬•▬•▬•

LOOKING AT MY LIFE—1

- *My Lifeline*

One way to determine how you have made decisions is to look at how your life has been shaped into its present form. Drawing a lifeline will help you do this. In the space provided on page 15 place dots showing how you felt (ranging from bad to good) about major events in your life. Figure 1 (page 14) shows Helen's lifeline. You may find it helpful to look at hers, although it may be very different from yours.

Now go back to your lifeline, and add the following marks:

! where you took the greatest risk of your life
For Helen this was when she decided to return to high school to graduate; she was frightened that it would be too hard, too awful.

X where an obstacle kept you from getting or doing what you wanted
Helen's pregnancy when she was only 16 prevented her from staying in school and led to the next point.

O where a critical decision was made for you by someone else
When Helen was pregnant, she was frightened and confused, so her mother and boyfriend, Pete, decided that the best thing was for Helen and Pete to get married.

— where you have made the worst decision of your life
Helen tried to save her marriage by having a second child. Looking back on it, she realized that that was not a good reason to have a child, and it certainly did not save the marriage. In fact, it seemed to make things worse.

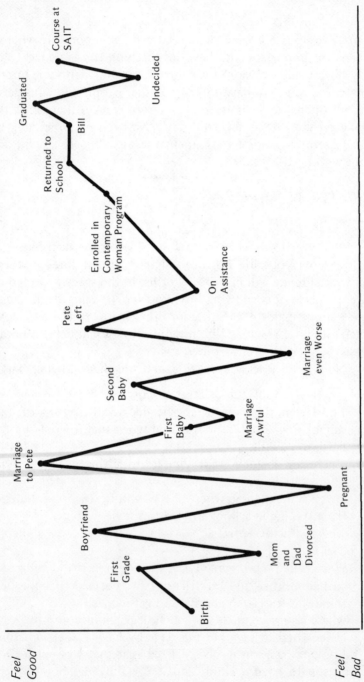

Figure 1. Helen's Lifeline

Feel
Good

Feel
Bad

MY LIFELINE

LOOKING AT MY LIFE—1 (continued)

+   where you have made the best decision of your life
     For Helen this was deciding to enroll in the Contemporary
     Woman program—the first step in controlling her own life.

?   where you see critical or important decisions coming up in
     the future
     Deciding what job to take after her 2-year course is com-
     pleted is a major decision Helen sees in the near future.
     She also feels she may have to make a decision about
     continuing or not continuing her relationship with the new
     man in her life, Bill. She is determined to make these
     decisions and not to drift into something by default nor to
     allow someone else to decide for her.

●━●━●━●

Having marked these events on your own lifeline, think
about how these decisions have affected your life. Your lifeline
may be more even than Helen's, it may have only a few peaks
and valleys, or it may have many. Did you actually make the
decisions that have affected your life? Many women have been
surprised to find that other people have made almost all the
large decisions for them. Some women find that they have never
had control over the decisions that have shaped their lives.
Someone else, like parents, friends, and husbands, has always
made the decision. Another surprising aspect has been realizing
what events contributed to feeling good or feeling bad. Child-
birth, which is often described as a most fulfilling part of a
woman's life, has been a negative experience for many women
who find they feel very trapped and enclosed.

Decision making may have seemed to be a reasoned or a
haphazard process for you. Psychologists have outlined logical
steps which can be used as a model for making well-considered
decisions. These steps help you consider all important aspects of
a decision. Such a logical, thorough approach to decision making is helpful when you are trying to make realistic decisions
about yourself and your future. Often the situation seems so
complex that it is discouraging. By following a logical, rational
process, however, you can handle this complexity.

One thing to remember in deciding about your future is

that *you are in charge* of the decisions to be made. You may seek help, advice, information, and support from other people and sources, but the final decision *must* be made by you.

STEPS OF THE PROCESS

The decision-making process can be divided into six steps:

1. defining the decision to be made
2. gathering relevant information
3. evaluating the information
4. choosing possible alternatives based on Steps 2 and 3
5. taking action on your choices and plans
6. evaluating progress and reviewing the process

Defining the Decision to be Made

A decision point is a time when you become aware of a specific situation and feel the need to make a decision about it. Through circumstances, for example, desertion or unexpected divorce, some women may be forced to change and to make decisions. Other women reach a point of feeling restless and in need of doing something different. Whatever your situation, you must be able to define the concern before you can solve it. What do you want or need to make a decision about?

LOOKING AT MY LIFE—2

*   *My Question*

Possibly the current question for you is, "Do I want to change?" or "How can I change to make my life more satisfying?" or "I am forced to change. Where do I start, what do I do?" or "What careers are best for me to consider?" or "Should I go to school or take a job?" Take some time to consider what your problem or question is. Consider it carefully to make sure you have the right one. Now try to word your concern or problem as a question in the most specific words you can find. Write it in the space provided.

_____

_____

LOOKING AT MY LIFE—2 (continued)

The question is written. Now the decision to be made is defined, and you are ready for the next step.

•━••━••━•

Gathering Relevant Information

This step in decision making involves two major activities: outlining all the major aspects about you and your situation as it is now and outlining all possible alternatives that should be considered.

Some areas to consider for this type of decision include: Who are you; what are your values, abilities, interests, and experiences; what are your present responsibilities; what are your personal needs; what are the workable alternatives in your community; and what are your personal and economic resources? These aspects will be more fully dealt with in the next chapters to help you consider each area.

Expansion is a key concept for this step in decision making. This means you need to forget about critical judgment for a short time while you generate many thoughts and ideas. Being as creative and/or as crazy as possible is important during this step. Assessment and evaluation, or judgment, of the ideas and alternatives generated occur at the next step. For now let yourself go. An idea that first seems impractical or silly may prove to be just the right solution when actually weighed in the light of other information.

Evaluating the Information

Sifting and sorting the information you have gathered occurs in this step. You weigh and evaluate the facts. As this occurs, some workable alternatives usually begin to emerge. Later you can consider each alternative with all the advantages and disadvantages that you are noting here in Step 3.

Choosing Possible Alternatives

The best alternatives that emerged during Step 3 are each seriously considered in Step 4. At this point it is important to consider positive and negative consequences associated with the alternatives. From the alternatives open to you, select the one or two which seem appropriate. Then outline the various actions necessary to achieve the appropriate alternatives.

Taking Action

With the hard work done, you now put into practice the plan you outlined to achieve your chosen alternative. This may seem to be the last step, but the next one is very important and should not be omitted.

Evaluating Progress and Reviewing the Process

In this step you review and re-evaluate your choice and plans at regular intervals. It is important to check to make sure your decision continues to be the best one possible. New information and new experiences may make it necessary for you to review your present decision. It may mean that you will decide to alter your plans slightly or even move to a different alternative. Reviewing has an added advantage: It keeps the reasons for your choice clear. It will show you that the decision-making process results in sound plans, and you will realize that you have logical reasons for making your decisions. This, just by itself, can provide a major confidence boost.

EXPLANATION OF THE PROCESS

Realizing how you or someone else might go through this decision-making process may be difficult to visualize. It sounds good in the abstract, but how does a real, live everyday person use the steps? To make each step clear and put it into a more concrete form, we have presented many examples throughout the book. The women in the examples are real. Some are single; some are single parents; some are married; some are separated or divorced. The idea of the examples is to help you see how other women have used the process. From this you will have a better idea of how to use each step for yourself.

If the situation in the example is not quite like yours, do read it anyway and try to see how the woman has used the process. Remember, the process is the important kernel to be gleaned from each example. For instance, even though you are a single parent raising four children and the example is about a married woman with one child, the process can be useful to you, although your solution may be different. Certainly there are differences in circumstances, but using the process is actually very similar for everyone.

To allow you to see the pattern of the process, one woman, Barbara, is used as a continuous example throughout the book. Her thoughts and experiences are added to by others' experiences of using the same process under different circumstances. This will also illustrate the individuality that is necessary; each woman must use the principles to reach her own unique decision.

Various women will be introduced to you throughout the book. We would like you to meet Barbara, who is a 38-year-old woman. She has been married for 18 years and has three children: two sons, Mark, 16, and Bill, 8; and one daughter, Susan, who is 14. When Barbara married, she had completed high school and nurse's training. Looking back at that particular time of her life, Barbara said:

> My parents felt that I should have some training to fall back on and urged me to go into nursing because I like people and it was a good "insurance-policy" occupation. My high school counselor suggested nursing, teaching, secretarial work, or university. Most of these seemed vague, except I had a friend whose sister was a nurse. Also I was elected president of the Future Nurses Club so decided that I'd better follow through.
>
> I hated nursing immediately, but this gorgeous man, Paul, came into my life. That was a neat experience, and I was having a great time socially, so I stayed in nursing. Paul and I were engaged in my third year of training and got married soon after my graduation. I worked as a nurse in a hospital for about 18 months until I began to "show" with our first baby.
>
> After that I stayed home and really fit myself into the wife-mother role: washing diapers, making brownies, swapping recipes with the neighbors, etc. I was very well organized, the way I thought I should be. One hundred percent of the responsibility of raising the children was mine. In the meantime Paul was advancing in his work and seemed to be working 24 hours a day. At the time we both felt this was how a marriage should be.

When Mark, my older son, went to school, I felt a slight sinking feeling but didn't know what it was. I became more involved in the community: den mother for Cubs, PTA, church work. The same sinking feeling occurred two years later when Susan entered school, and I seemed to have lots of time on my hands. It was the first inkling that I needed to DO SOME-THING. I wondered what I would do with all the time and considered returning to work as a nurse. However, hospital shift work didn't seem to fit very well with raising a young family, office nurse positions were considered "plums" and hard to find, and I felt my training was out of date. Who would want to hire an old married woman of 28? The process was simplified when I realized that I was pregnant again.

Looking back, I think I was relieved that I could slip back into being a wife and mother. I didn't have to face the outside world or myself. However, when Bill was 3, I began to wonder what I would do when he was also in school. I talked with friends about how I felt. Some couldn't understand my concern in planning for when I was 36, 38, 40, or more. Their advice was to just relax, enjoy my children and my freedom. I deserved it. But what was I going to do for the next 20 years as my children got older and more independent and my husband was wrapped up in his work? Other friends had similar feelings but also weren't sure what to do. By this time I was pretty sure I didn't want to return to nursing. I had had enough of taking care of people since I had nursed three children through measles, chicken pox, colds, flu, stomach aches, and the sniffles. But what else could I do?

I heard about a women's club and decided to join. It was a group all for me! I was so darn busy when the children were small—exhausted from just coping with all the demands—that I had no time for me. I didn't consider that I had needs. The club was the beginning of my awakening as a person, an individual.

Then one day a friend called and mentioned a course that was advertised in the paper, Contemporary Woman: Options and Opportunities. *It sounded like it might be just the thing to help me decide. The course was the first time that I really considered what I wanted to do with the rest of my life. Until*

*the course I hadn't considered my opportunities because I just
didn't think there were any for me.*

Barbara is just one example. She will reappear throughout
the book to show how one woman used this process for herself.
Other women's experiences will also be described to illustrate
other alternatives and situations. Barbara and the other women
are presented as examples and role models, not as "This is what
you should do!" *You are the only person who can decide what
you want and what is best for you. There is no surefire blue-
print for you to assume from the examples. You are your own
best expert on yourself, and by following the decision-making
process outlined in the book you can feel confident in your
ability to decide.*

Does this seem like a long, burdensome procedure? It does
involve a lot of effort, soul-searching, and time. During the
process there will probably be times when you will feel discouraged: It takes too long and it is too confusing. Stick with it, for
there will also probably be times of great joy and elation, a
"eureka" feeling. The end result of a logical, carefully thought
through decision with a considered plan of action will be well
worth the trouble. The confidence you can then feel in yourself
will be a tremendous asset. Remember, you are making a critical
life decision that deserves great care. Decision making can also
be fun as you discover new things about yourself and piece the
puzzle together.

Three
Who Am I?

IDENTITY PROBLEMS

Many women feel as if they have lost their identity. Others feel as if they have never really had a chance to find themselves as individuals. Perhaps you share this frustration. The circumstances leading to the feeling are often very different for various persons, but the feeling for most is very similar.

Kathy had been knocked from pillar to post as a child. She married when she was 17, had a baby, and was deserted by her husband after 3 years. Kathy had not finished school, had few marketable skills, but had to get a job to support herself and her child. She now works as a waitress at night and on weekends. She has not had time to really consider who she is or what she would like to become. There has not been time to consider a long-term plan.

On the other hand, Barbara feels as if she has lost herself taking care of her family's needs and desires. Her own needs have inadvertently slipped to the end of a long string where they are seldom considered. She, too, has not had time to really consider who she is or what she would like to do differently to feel more satisfied.

For these reasons and others like them, it is vital to ask seriously and honestly the question, "Who am I?" It is important to take time to get in touch with yourself and to consider your own unique needs.

In this chapter there are a number of questions and written exercises which are designed to help you examine yourself as a person: how you view yourself, how others see you, how you spend your time, what you are interested in, what is important to you, and so on. This is the first part of gathering the relevant information necessary for decision making. Although some of the items may seem trivial or too basic, carefully complete each item of this personal inventory. Weigh each question and answer for possible advantage or disadvantage in terms of your changing.

•◄■•◄■•◄■•

LOOKING AT MY LIFE—3

- *Basic Information*

Fill in the following blanks.

My name is _____

I am _____ years old.

My health is usually

_____ excellent
_____ good
_____ fair
_____ poor

If you answered fair or poor, list the reasons and state how this limits you.

1. _____
2. _____
3. _____

•◄■•◄■•◄■•

LOOKING AT MY LIFE—4

- *I Am Statements*

Here are 10 statements that begin with I am. Complete all 10, each with a different ending.

1. I am _____
2. I am _____
3. I am _____
4. I am _____
5. I am _____
6. I am _____
7. I am _____
8. I am _____

9. I am _____
10. I am _____

How have you described yourself: by roles, feelings, personal qualities, physical appearance, skills, goals, other things? What characteristics have emerged or have you emphasized?

•━━•━━•━━•

LOOKING AT MY LIFE—5

• *I Wish I Were Statements*

Now complete 10 statements beginning with I wish I were:

1. I wish I were _____
2. I wish I were _____
3. I wish I were _____
4. I wish I were _____
5. I wish I were _____
6. I wish I were _____
7. I wish I were _____
8. I wish I were _____
9. I wish I were _____
10. I wish I were _____

•━━•━━•━━•

LOOKING AT MY LIFE—6

• *Conclusions about Myself*

What have you emphasized in your I Wish I Were Statements: roles, feelings, personal qualities, physical appearance, skills, goals, other things? What are the differences between what you are and what you want to become? Go back over your I Am Statements and put a star beside characteristics or behavior you want to keep or strengthen. Review your I Wish I Were Statements; star characteristics you would like to develop.

•━━•━━•━━•

LOOKING AT MY LIFE—7

• *My Description of Myself*

Now take another approach. Look at the list of words in the first part of this exercise. Read each word and decide if it describes you. Place a check beside those words you consider to be characteristic of you. Such adjectives can help you review your self-image and get a more balanced view of yourself.

LOOKING AT MY LIFE—7 (continued)

You may want to have friends or members of your family also describe you with this list and then compare the lists. This is a good method and a good time to obtain others' impressions of you.

*ADJECTIVE CHECK-LIST**

__ able	__ flexible	__ progressive
__ academic	__ forceful	__ prudent
__ accurate	__ formal	__ purposeful
__ adaptable	__ frank	__ quick
__ adventurous	__ friendly	__ quiet
__ affectionate	__ generous	__ rational
__ aggressive	__ gentle	__ realistic
__ alert	__ good-natured	__ reasonable
__ ambitious	__ healthy	__ reflective
__ artistic	__ helpful	__ relaxed
__ assertive	__ honest	__ reliable
__ attractive	__ humorous	__ reserved
__ bold	__ idealistic	__ resourceful
__ broad-minded	__ imaginative	__ responsible
__ businesslike	__ independent	__ retiring
__ calm	__ individualistic	__ robust
__ capable	__ industrious	__ self-confident
__ careful	__ informal	__ self-controlled
__ cautious	__ ingenious	__ sensible
__ charming	__ intellectual	__ sensitive
__ cheerful	__ intelligent	__ serious
__ clear-thinking	__ inventive	__ sharp-witted
__ clever	__ kind	__ sincere
__ competent	__ leisurely	__ sociable
__ confident	__ light-hearted	__ spontaneous
__ conscientious	__ likable	__ spunky
__ conservative	__ logical	__ stable
__ considerate	__ loyal	__ steady

*Adapted from Miriam H. Krohn. *Planning for Work.* New York: Catalyst, 1973, pp. 20-21. The adaptation is repeated twice in this chapter.

___ cool
___ cooperative
___ courageous
___ creative
___ curious
___ daring
___ deliberate
___ democratic
___ dependable
___ determined
___ dignified
___ discreet
___ dominant
___ eager
___ easy-going
___ efficient
___ emotional
___ energetic
___ enterprising
___ enthusiastic
___ fair-minded
___ farsighted
___ firm

___ mature
___ methodical
___ meticulous
___ mild
___ moderate
___ modest
___ natural
___ obliging
___ open-minded
___ opportunistic
___ optimistic
___ organized
___ original
___ outgoing
___ painstaking
___ patient
___ peaceable
___ persevering
___ pleasant
___ poised
___ polite
___ practical
___ precise

___ strong
___ strong-minded
___ sympathetic
___ tactful
___ teachable
___ tenacious
___ thorough
___ thoughtful
___ tolerant
___ tough
___ trusting
___ trustworthy
___ unaffected
___ unassuming
___ understanding
___ unexcitable
___ uninhibited
___ verbal
___ versatile
___ warm
___ wholesome
___ wise
___ witty
___ zany

Write below other words that describe you.

_____   _____   _____
_____   _____   _____
_____   _____   _____
_____   _____   _____
_____   _____   _____
_____   _____   _____

Now look back over the list and group the words together into similar characteristics to pinpoint your strengths. For example, you might have checked ambitious, competitive, assertive, forceful, etc., which could all fit into a category. Affectionate, friendly, kind, and outgoing have similarities which could form another category.

LOOKING AT MY LIFE–7 (continued)

Space is provided for you to decide on a summary title for the characteristics that fall into a group. Your title may be one of the characteristics or another word altogether. For instance, Barbara grouped gentle, kind, sensitive, sympathetic, trusting, warm, understanding, and thoughtful into a category *caring*.

This part will give you a clearer picture of your self-image.

	I	II	III
Characteristics:	1. _____	1. _____	1. _____
	2. _____	2. _____	2. _____
	3. _____	3. _____	3. _____
	4. _____	4. _____	4. _____
	5. _____	5. _____	5. _____
	6. _____	6. _____	6. _____
Summary Title:	_____	_____	_____

LOOKING AT MY LIFE–8

- *A Male's Description of Me*

Now have your *husband or closest male friend* complete this list.

ADJECTIVE CHECK-LIST

Check the characteristics which you feel best describe _____ .

__ able	__ flexible	__ progressive
__ academic	__ forceful	__ prudent
__ accurate	__ formal	__ purposeful
__ adaptable	__ frank	__ quick
__ adventurous	__ friendly	__ quiet
__ affectionate	__ generous	__ rational
__ aggressive	__ gentle	__ realistic
__ alert	__ good-natured	__ reasonable
__ ambitious	__ healthy	__ reflective
__ artistic	__ helpful	__ relaxed
__ assertive	__ honest	__ reliable
__ attractive	__ humorous	__ reserved
__ bold	__ idealistic	__ resourceful

___ broad-minded
___ businesslike
___ calm
___ capable
___ careful
___ cautious
___ charming
___ cheerful
___ clear-thinking
___ clever
___ competent
___ confident
___ conscientious
___ conservative
___ considerate
___ cool
___ cooperative
___ courageous
___ creative
___ curious
___ daring
___ deliberate
___ democratic
___ dependable
___ determined
___ dignified
___ discreet
___ dominant
___ eager
___ easy-going
___ efficient
___ emotional
___ energetic
___ enterprising
___ enthusiastic
___ fair-minded
___ farsighted
___ firm

___ imaginative
___ independent
___ individualistic
___ industrious
___ informal
___ ingenious
___ intellectual
___ intelligent
___ inventive
___ kind
___ leisurely
___ light-hearted
___ likable
___ logical
___ loyal
___ mature
___ methodical
___ meticulous
___ mild
___ moderate
___ modest
___ natural
___ obliging
___ open-minded
___ opportunistic
___ optimistic
___ organized
___ original
___ outgoing
___ painstaking
___ patient
___ peaceable
___ persevering
___ pleasant
___ poised
___ polite
___ practical
___ precise

___ responsible
___ retiring
___ robust
___ self-confident
___ self-controlled
___ sensible
___ sensitive
___ serious
___ sharp-witted
___ sincere
___ sociable
___ spontaneous
___ spunky
___ stable
___ steady
___ strong
___ strong-minded
___ sympathetic
___ tactful
___ teachable
___ tenacious
___ thorough
___ thoughtful
___ tolerant
___ tough
___ trusting
___ trustworthy
___ unaffected
___ unassuming
___ understanding
___ unexcitable
___ uninhibited
___ verbal
___ versatile
___ warm
___ wholesome
___ wise
___ witty
___ zany

LOOKING AT MY LIFE—8 (continued)

Write below other words that describe her.

_____ _____ _____
_____ _____ _____
_____ _____ _____
_____ _____ _____
_____ _____ _____

●━●━●━●━●

LOOKING AT MY LIFE—9

- *Another Person's Description of Me*

Have someone else—for example, a trusted friend or relative who knows you well but may have a different perspective of you as a person—complete this list, checking those characteristics he or she feels best describe you.

ADJECTIVE CHECK-LIST

Check the characteristics that you feel best describe

_____ .

__ able	__ flexible	__ progressive
__ academic	__ forceful	__ prudent
__ accurate	__ formal	__ purposeful
__ adaptable	__ frank	__ quick
__ adventurous	__ friendly	__ quiet
__ affectionate	__ generous	__ rational
__ aggressive	__ gentle	__ realistic
__ alert	__ good-natured	__ reasonable
__ ambitious	__ healthy	__ reflective
__ artistic	__ helpful	__ relaxed
__ assertive	__ honest	__ reliable
__ attractive	__ humorous	__ reserved
__ bold	__ idealistic	__ resourceful
__ broad-minded	__ imaginative	__ responsible
__ businesslike	__ independent	__ retiring

___ calm
___ capable
___ careful
___ cautious
___ charming
___ cheerful
___ clear-thinking
___ clever
___ competent
___ confident
___ conscientious
___ conservative
___ considerate
___ cool
___ cooperative
___ courageous
___ creative
___ curious
___ daring
___ deliberate
___ democratic
___ dependable
___ determined
___ dignified
___ discreet
___ dominant
___ eager
___ easy-going
___ efficient
___ emotional
___ energetic
___ enterprising
___ enthusiastic
___ fair-minded
___ farsighted
___ firm

___ individualistic
___ industrious
___ informal
___ ingenious
___ intellectual
___ intelligent
___ inventive
___ kind
___ leisurely
___ light-hearted
___ likable
___ logical
___ loyal
___ mature
___ methodical
___ meticulous
___ mild
___ moderate
___ modest
___ natural
___ obliging
___ open-minded
___ opportunistic
___ optimistic
___ organized
___ original
___ outgoing
___ painstaking
___ patient
___ peaceable
___ persevering
___ pleasant
___ poised
___ polite
___ practical
___ precise

___ robust
___ self-confident
___ self-controlled
___ sensible
___ sensitive
___ serious
___ sharp-witted
___ sincere
___ sociable
___ spontaneous
___ spunky
___ stable
___ steady
___ strong
___ strong-minded
___ sympathetic
___ tactful
___ teachable
___ tenacious
___ thorough
___ thoughtful
___ tolerant
___ tough
___ trusting
___ trustworthy
___ unaffected
___ unassuming
___ understanding
___ unexcitable
___ uninhibited
___ verbal
___ versatile
___ warm
___ wholesome
___ wise
___ witty
___ zany

LOOKING AT MY LIFE—9 (continued)

Write below other words that describe her.

_____   _____   _____
_____   _____   _____
_____   _____   _____
_____   _____   _____
_____   _____   _____
_____   _____   _____

•➤•➤•➤•

LOOKING AT MY LIFE—10

• *My Description and Theirs*

Now take the check-lists others have filled in for you and do the grouping of characteristics as you did for your own list.

Categories as seen by my husband or closest male friend:

	I	II	III
Characteristics:	1. _____	1. _____	1. _____
	2. _____	2. _____	2. _____
	3. _____	3. _____	3. _____
	4. _____	4. _____	4. _____
	5. _____	5. _____	5. _____
	6. _____	6. _____	6. _____
Summary Title:	_____	_____	_____

Categories as seen by my best friend:

	I	II	III
Characteristics:	1. _____	1. _____	1. _____
	2. _____	2. _____	2. _____
	3. _____	3. _____	3. _____
	4. _____	4. _____	4. _____
	5. _____	5. _____	5. _____
	6. _____	6. _____	6. _____
Summary Title:	_____	_____	_____

How do the three summaries of personal adjectives compare? Are there similarities? Are there discrepancies? Discuss the lists with those people who filled them out and discover what categories and titles they would use.

Which categories would they use?

_____

_____

_____

How are they the same or different from yours?

_____

_____

_____

If there are differences, discover what about you or their perception of you has caused the differences.

It is common for a woman to find that she has emphasized what she sees as negative adjectives and has almost ignored the positive ones, even though others have checked many of these.

Joan discovered that her best female friend and her male friend had checked very similar adjectives. They saw her as able, calm, intelligent, optimistic, resourceful, self-confident, and spunky. Joan was surprised that these two very different people had such similar perceptions of her. What is more their perceptions were different from her own! Of their similar list she had only checked intelligent.

In other cases a woman may feel she is very organized, but her husband views her as scattered and disorganized. Isabel found she was highly organized with her children, her own work, and her outside activities, but when something involved her husband, she tended to leave it up to him. He thus mistakenly had the feeling she was scattered. This was important information to have discovered about herself. The differences in viewpoints can lead you to valuable information about yourself.

VALUES VERSUS TIME USE

Another kind of basic information you need to look at is your values. They are usually implied (sometimes buried) in what you do and what you want to do. It is difficult to set out your values specifically. People often just assume values must be there. However, it is helpful in most decision making to spend time naming and considering them.

Lifestyles are basically *behaviors* in which you engage to live out your values and beliefs.[1] Your lifestyle is your overall way of looking at the world and how you behave in relation to other people, your physical environment, ideas, and yourself. Therefore, you need to know what is important to you and what your values are. You do not choose your values in a simple manner. They develop and change throughout your lifetime. Your childhood and later experiences and training, your intellectual awareness, your emotional responsiveness, and your physical endowment contribute to the development of your values. You apply your values in many settings, activities, and relationships—at home, at work, and in leisure; in educational, recreational, volunteer, or community undertakings. You probably find all of these activities satisfying and fulfilling when they reflect your basic values. When you feel uneasy, there is likely some conflict between your values and your behavior. Bringing your behavior back in line with your values can help you feel happier and more fulfilled. More importantly, you can make choices that reflect your value orientation, and *these choices can then reflect your own uniqueness.*

•➤•➤•➤•

LOOKING AT MY LIFE—11

• *My Values*

Consider for a few minutes what your values are. To help you summarize them, complete the following statements.

For me, I value _____

_____

_____

_____

For my family, I value _____

_____

_____

_____

•➤•➤•➤•

It may help you to see that Barbara summarized her personal values in the following way.

For me, I value:
- learning more about myself, how I relate to others and they to me, and most important, learning to like and accept me, warts and all!
- a secure and stable base so that I can appreciate and develop myself as an individual.
- involvement with other people as well as being independent; interdependence is very important to me.
- achievement which meets my need for accomplishment, challenge, and recognition.

For my family, I value:

- their right to choose their own values and to live them in whatever way is satisfying to themselves. I expect my children have or will have some of my values, but I hope that they feel free to develop their own.

CATEGORIES OF VALUES

In attempting to understand people, psychologists have considered different dimensions and strengths of values or needs.[2] Some are described in terms of relating to others; some, in terms of relating to yourself. Described briefly are those values that most often seem relevant to women. Each person usually has a mixture of these values and needs, with certain ones being stronger than others. Please note that the values or needs are listed alphabetically to help eliminate any message that some are more important or better than others.

Values and Needs in Relating to People

Achievement. A value or need to do your best, to be successful by determination and hard work. This may include assuming or accepting more and more responsibility.

Belonging. A value or need to feel accepted and friendly with other people. Approval from others is important as well as a feeling that you are being treated like a person and that you give something to the relationship. Doing things with friends is preferred to being alone.

Esteem. A value or need to be a leader in groups and to be regarded by others as a leader. To be able to influence, persuade, and/or control others is important. You would like to gain admiration, publicity, important friends, and/or wealth.

Following. A value or need to get suggestions, instructions, and/or leadership from others. It is important to do what is expected and to avoid the unconventional. You would prefer to have someone else make the decisions.

Helpfulness. A value or need to help others who are ill or in trouble. Generosity and affection are two important aspects. For example, you do various things for people and perhaps listen to their personal problems.

Independence. A value or need for freedom and the opportunity to control your own life so that you can develop new ideas and operate differently from others. This may involve being independent of others in making decisions and doing things that are unconventional.

Power. A value or need to be influential, take initiative, make decisions, and be in a position of leadership. Feelings of competence and confidence are important. This value might be expressed in relationships or in work with organizations.

Intrapersonal Values or Needs

Change or Risk. A value or need to experience new and different things. This may range from eating new and different foods to enjoying activities that involve excitement, pressure, and even emergencies. It is important to experience novelty and change in a daily routine.

Creativity. A value or need to have the freedom to use your imagination, ideas, and ability to create.

Introspection. A value or need to analyze your own motives and feelings and to understand other people's feelings. This may also involve wanting to predict how others will act.

Knowledge. A value or need to satisfy your curiosity and increase your knowledge by continued formal and informal learning. This may include enjoyment in accumulating and recording information.

Order. A value or need to have things organized and neat, to have a well thought out plan before beginning a difficult task. It is important to have things planned and arranged so that they run smoothly, preferably without change.

Personal Satisfaction. A value or need to be involved in activities that you like very much and which provide more personal than financial rewards. This includes having pride in what you do and having others recognize what you do as important.

Security. A value or need for a stable base that leaves you relatively free from emotional stress and worry.

Personal Preferences

One other aspect to include here is a personal preference rather than a value. Often in analyzing the content of jobs, it is important to determine whether a person prefers working with data, people, or things.[3]

Data Orientation. Indicates that a person prefers activities where she deals with information, knowledge, and concepts. Such functions as synthesizing, coordinating, analyzing, computing, copying, comparing, and compiling might be done in relationship to the data.

People Orientation. Indicates that a person prefers activi-

ties which involve working with people. This may involve discussing, instructing, serving, supervising, negotiating, and/or persuading.

Things Orientation. Indicates that a person prefers activities which involve making or working with physical objects.
This usually involves working mostly with your hands and may
include enjoying the results of the work being seen by others.

•▬•▬•▬•

LOOKING AT MY LIFE—12

- *Order of my Values*

To add to your information about your personal values
and needs, try to rank order those listed in each category.

Things I value in relating to people: achievement, belonging, esteem, following, helpfulness, independence, and power.

Value Most   1. _____
                  2. _____
                  3. _____
                  4. _____
                  5. _____
                  6. _____
Value Least   7. _____

Things I value for me: change, creativity, introspection,
knowledge, order, personal satisfaction, and security.

Value Most   1. _____
                  2. _____
                  3. _____
                  4. _____
                  5. _____
                  6. _____
Value Least   7. _____

Of the data, people, and things orientation, I personally

Prefer Most   1. _____
                  2. _____
Prefer Least   3. _____

•▬•▬•▬•

Barbara's rank ordering of her values in relating to people was:

Value Most   1. independence
                          2. belonging
                          3. achievement
                          4. helpfulness
                          5. esteem
                          6. following
Value Least   7. power

For the things she valued for herself, she ordered her values as:

Value Most   1. introspection
                          2. personal satisfaction
                          3. security
                          4. change or risk
                          5. knowledge
                          6. creativity
Value Least   7. order

One thing Barbara found in this exercise was that the order of her values had changed a great deal. Previously she would have ranked *order* very near the top.

LOOKING AT MY LIFE—13

● *My Activities*

A critical aspect for happiness and satisfaction is how well your values are displayed in your behavior and in your use of time. In this section you will have an opportunity to check this aspect.

One good method for analyzing your time use follows. First, keep a diary for one week, noting what you do during each hour. A chart is included on page 40 to make it easy for you. Do not change what you would usually do but simply observe your own actions and record them. Be specific enough about your activities that you can review and remember your time use by looking at the chart.

TIME SCHEDULE

(Be deliberate about making plans.)

Name _____   Week of _____

	MON	TUES	WED	THUR	FRI	SAT	SUN
6-7							
7-8							
8-9							
9-10							
10-11							
11-12							
12-1							
1-2							
2-3							
3-4							
4-5							
5-6							
6-7							
7-8							
8-9							
9-10							
10-11							
11-12							

LOOKING AT MY LIFE—13 (continued)

Second, at the end of the week, review your schedule. Do some activities take more or less time than you thought? How do you feel about how you spend your time? What changes can you suggest from looking at your time schedule? Which activities are essential and which are done more out of choice?

Third, after thinking through these questions, make out a projected diary for the next week. (You may reproduce the Time Schedule chart for your own use.)

Fourth, keep a diary of your real use of time that week. Make notes to account for the difference in your real use of time and your planned schedule. What have you learned about your use of time? Use what you have learned to plan the third week in this analysis, and again watch your actual time use. Continue this process as long as you continue to learn from it. This information about your schedule will also be useful in Chapter Four.

When you look back over your time schedule and see how you have used your time, do you find that your time use is consistent with your values? Or are some of your important values not reflected in the way you spend your time? Keeping track and asking these questions has helped many women realize how little time they have actually used for themselves and what they value.

Jan is a woman who used this method to learn about her own use of time. She always felt busy and pushed, and as a wife and mother of three as well as part-time university student, she does have a full life. She learned that she must allow more flexibility in her days. Jan had overscheduled herself and became rattled when something unexpected arose for her to deal with. She had allowed no contingency time, no room to fit in either emergencies or unexpected pleasures like having coffee with a friend she chanced to meet on campus. To use this new learning, she had to work a value for more flexibility into her actual use of time so that she would stop overscheduling herself.

LOOKING AT MY LIFE—14

• *Possible Changes in my Activities*

Using your values and your time schedule, look at the following Activities List and fill in what activities you might like to add. Also think about and list what activities you would like to increase, decrease, eliminate, or keep in your life. Write the activity in the appropriate column.

In doing these exercises, you can begin to see what keeps you from using your time according to the values you have listed for yourself. What gets in your way? Often the answer focuses on everyday tasks and responsibilities that seem to be imposed by others, for example, cooking, cleaning, doing committee activities, working overtime, being a hostess, and caring for children. It is important to ask, "Am *I* doing things that prevent me from realizing my values in my activities?" Answering this question may help you to accept responsibility for allowing other people to saddle you with tasks or to accept responsibility for sitting back and watching life pass by. Not deciding and not acting is making a choice. Joanne Woodward recently said, "I've spent too many years saying that I'm afraid to try new things. It's time I started grabbing things I want from life. For too many years I've put off taking advantage of the incredible experiences that life has to offer."[4]

LOOKING AT MY LIFE—15

• *My Learnings**

This has been a long, but important, chapter in sorting out some basic information about you: I Am and I Wish I Were Statements in combination with descriptive adjectives, activities, and values of your present lifestyle as well as a summary of your values for yourself and for others. Thinking back over

---

*Adapted from Sidney B. Simon. Values clarification: A tool for counsellors. *Personnel and Guidance Journal*, 1973, *51* (9), 617. This adaptation is also used in Chapters Four, Five, Six, Seven, and Eight.

ACTIVITIES LIST

Add	Increase	Decrease	Eliminate	Keep

LOOKING AT MY LIFE—15 (continued)

these things, focus on what you have learned in this chapter by completing the following sentences:

I learned that I _____

_____

I relearned that I _____

_____

I became aware _____

_____

I was surprised _____

_____

I was pleased _____

_____

I was disappointed _____

_____

I see that I need to _____

_____

I _____

_____

I _____

_____

SUGGESTED READING

Bernard, Jessie. *Women, wives, mothers: values and options.* Chicago: Aldine Publishing, 1975.

Jessie Bernard examines the dramatic changes in values being experienced by women of all ages in all classes of society and how these changes are affecting the options available to you today. She systematically reviews research on sex differences and different developmental periods women experience.

Halas, Celia, & Matteson, Roberta. *I've done so well—why do I feel so bad?* New York: Macmillan, 1978.

The authors feel you, as a woman in our society, have received confusing, self-contradictory, and absurd messages throughout your life. These paradoxes can be baffling, for example: be aggressive and passive, be self-centered and selfless, be a madonna and a tramp. Often the messages cause conflict with your own inner desires for happiness, success, and fulfillment. The authors help you recognize and resolve the confusing and destructive messages you receive at home, in school, or at work.

Jongeward, Dorothy, & Scott, Dru. *Women as winners.* New York: Addison-Wesley, 1977.

This book opens up new areas for women to consider. The authors help you become more aware of your strengths, show you how to recognize and achieve goals, and indicate how you can have more fun.

Rogers, Carl. *Becoming a person.* Austin, TX: The Hogg Foundation, 1956.

This brief pamphlet contains two lectures presented by Dr. Carl Rogers in 1954. The first describes how personal growth can be encouraged, and the second deals with what it means to become a person. Rogers feels that being a person is a fluid, ongoing process, in which a person continually discovers new aspects of herself in the flow of experience.

Sargent, Alice G. *Beyond sex roles.* New York: West Publishing, 1977.

The author presents a series of exercises and readings to help you engage in

SUGGESTED READING (continued)

self-exploration, reflection, and introspection to discover which attitudes and behaviors are sex-role related. This can lead to awareness of which sex-role expectations inhibit you and how to begin changing and letting go of a few of the role inhibitions.

Schmidt, Jerry A. *Help yourself: a guide to self-change.* Champaign, IL: Research Press, 1976.

Basic principles involved in changing yourself are described in this book. Then specific strategies helpful in bringing about your desired change are discussed and applied to your situation.

Sheehy, Gail. *Passages: predictable crises of adult life.* New York: Bantam Books, 1976.

The author discusses adult life stages, pointing out the personality and sexual changes which occur. The emphasis is on using each life stage and/ or crisis as an opportunity for creative change and growth.

Four
What Have I Done?

EDUCATIONAL AND WORK EXPERIENCES

This chapter helps you consider the resources you have gained from your experiences. Often your experiences shape what the future will be, but more importantly, they provide valuable information for you to consider in finding the best future alternative for you. These experiences may have developed out of formal or informal classes, committee work, personal accomplishments, and reading. You may have developed talents, interests, and skills of which you are not aware. This is the case for many women. When you do become aware of these assets, you may feel like down playing them as rusty, ancient history of no importance now. Don't you believe it! There is much information available in your history that could be most useful to the decision at hand. Finding it is another part of gathering the relevant information to make the best decision.

The experiences that will be reviewed in this chapter are your educational background; work experience, both paid and unpaid; and interests. The next chapter is concerned with your present situation; if you are now primarily a wife and mother, you will review these experiences in that chapter.

You may not have had some experiences which are covered in this chapter. Briefly skim those sections, gleaning any information you can, but concentrate most on the sections which apply to you.

The purpose of looking at your educational background has two main thrusts: first, to have you assess your formal education, your likes and dislikes in school, and the activities related to academic work; second, to have you assess your informal educational experiences, which may add much to the picture.

LOOKING AT MY LIFE—16

- *My Educational Background*

In thinking about your formal education, you may begin to feel sensitive or discouraged. These feelings may arise when you think that your education, no matter of what it consisted or when you took it, is irrelevant and outdated. Skills are rusty and knowledge is vague. Most women do feel that way at this stage. However, you need to look at what useful information is available by assessing that old education to see what you have accomplished, what interests continue, what skills you have developed, and what can now be put to use. Fill in these blanks.

High School

I completed Grade _____ in 19 _____

While in school, I liked:

Subjects (for example, Chemistry):

1. _____
2. _____
3. _____
4. _____
5. _____

Activities (for example, I enjoyed doing experiments but did not like writing them up):

1. _____
2. _____
3. _____
4. _____
5. _____

Other:

1. _____
2. _____
3. _____
4. _____
5. _____

While in school I disliked:

Subjects:

1. _____
2. _____
3. _____
4. _____
5. _____

Activities:

1. _____
2. _____
3. _____
4. _____
5. _____

Other:

1. _____
2. _____
3. _____
4. _____
5. _____

From High School, the experiences I value most are:

1. _____
2. _____
3. _____
4. _____
5. _____

Further Training

Dates:

Secretarial: _____
Nursing: _____
Junior College: _____
University: _____
Technical: _____
Other: _____

LOOKING AT MY LIFE—16 (continued)

While getting my further training I liked:

Subjects:

1. _____
2. _____
3. _____
4. _____
5. _____

Activities:

1. _____
2. _____
3. _____
4. _____
5. _____

Other:

1. _____
2. _____
3. _____
4. _____
5. _____

While getting my further training I disliked:

Subjects:

1. _____
2. _____
3. _____
4. _____
5. _____

Activities:

1. _____
2. _____
3. _____
4. _____

5. _____

    Other:

1. _____
2. _____
3. _____
4. _____
5. _____

From my further training, I value most:

1. _____
2. _____
3. _____
4. _____
5. _____

Informal Education

(This includes activities or experiences from which you have learned facts, gained new knowledge, and/or developed self-awareness.)

    Classes:

1. _____
2. _____
3. _____

    Reading:

1. _____
2. _____
3. _____

    Workshops:

1. _____
2. _____
3. _____

    Other:

1. _____
2. _____
3. _____

LOOKING AT MY LIFE—16 (continued)

The things I liked in my informal education were:

1. _____
2. _____
3. _____
4. _____
5. _____

The things I disliked in my informal education were:

1. _____
2. _____
3. _____
4. _____
5. _____

From my informal education I value most:

1. _____
2. _____
3. _____
4. _____
5. _____

Interests Continued and Characteristics Developed

I have maintained my interest in parts of my education by (Specify how and what.):

Reading:

1. _____
2. _____
3. _____

Practicing:

1. _____
2. _____
3. _____

Belonging to professional associations:

1. _____
2. _____
3. _____

Other:

1. _____
2. _____
3. _____

I still particularly like the following about my education:

1. _____
2. _____
3. _____

and would like to pursue further (for example, organization, writing skills):

1. _____
2. _____

The most important personal characteristics that I developed throughout my education were:

1. _____
2. _____
3. _____
4. _____
5. _____

—•—•—•—•

LOOKING AT MY LIFE—17

- *My Work Experiences*

Your work experiences also may seem like ancient history or be nonexistent. However, it is important to look for the valuable information concerning likes, dislikes, and personal characteristics that were involved with different positions that you have held. Take some time now to write this information

LOOKING AT MY LIFE—17 (continued)

on the following pages. Remember to include part-time and summer jobs as well as any full-time experiences you have had. It is not uncommon for women to find that work they did when they were 16 had many characteristics that they would like to find in a job now. There is also a section on volunteer or unpaid work. This may reveal some interesting aspects too.

You may decide to use your earlier experiences as a base for the future or, on the other hand, you may wish to junk them and start afresh. These are only two of many possibilities, given to show that it is important to cover all aspects so that you feel comfortable with the alternative you eventually choose.

Paid Work Experiences

I have had experience in the following jobs:

Job	*Duties*	*Dates*
1.		
2.		
3.		
4.		
5.		

I most enjoyed my work as _____

What I liked about this job was:

1. _____
2. _____
3. _____

I least enjoyed my work as _____

What I disliked about this job was:

1. _____
2. _____
3. _____

The personal characteristics (for example, sense of responsibility, efficiency) which helped me in my work were:

1. _____
2. _____
3. _____
4. _____
5. _____

The personal characteristics (for example, personality clashes with coworkers, tardiness) which hindered me in work were:

1. _____
2. _____
3. _____
4. _____
5. _____

The skills I gained in these jobs were:

1. _____
2. _____
3. _____
4. _____
5. _____

Volunteer Work Experiences

Your work as a volunteer can provide you with valuable skills. Be generous in giving yourself credit for what you accomplished, your methods, and experience.

I have done the following work as a volunteer:

Organization	Tasks	Dates
1.		

LOOKING AT MY LIFE—17 (continued)

Organization	Tasks	Dates

2. _____

3. _____

4. _____

5. _____

I most enjoyed my work as _____

What I liked about this work was:

1. _____
2. _____
3. _____

I least enjoyed my work as _____

What I disliked about this work was:

1. _____
2. _____
3. _____

The personal characteristics which helped me in volunteer work were:

1. _____
2. _____
3. _____

The personal characteristics which hindered me in volunteer work were:

1. _____
2. _____
3. _____

The skills I gained in completing these tasks were:

1. _____
2. _____
3. _____

●━●━●━●

INTERESTS

So far in this chapter you have been cataloging past experiences, looking for threads that will provide a structure for your decision. In this section, you will be looking at more specific activities that you can do already or that you would like to do. The last category is very important! What you would like to do and/or what you have some curiosity about or interest in can be crucial factors to consider. While you are thinking of these interests, try not to censor them with, "I couldn't do that now" or "I don't have any talent or ability for that," or other such negative thoughts.

●━●━●━●

LOOKING AT MY LIFE—18

• *My Categories of Interests*

While completing the following exercise, dream a little to ensure that you note all the possible activities and interests which you can or would like to do. Be sure also to consider the activities and interests you had when you were 12 or 13. Research on women's life patterns seems to indicate that those earlier interests get put underground for many years but often re-emerge and have value.[1]

Categories of realistic, investigative, artistic, social, and leadership are supplied here to help you order your activities and interests.[2] Are you ready to think and dream a little?

Realistic

This category includes activities and interests that involve doing concrete things with tools leading to a finished end product that often is visible. Some examples are typing 40 w.p.m., using wood-shop power tools, driving a car, completing a tax return, and climbing to the top of a mountain.

LOOKING AT MY LIFE—18 (continued)

I can do and like doing the following *realistic* activities:

1. _____
2. _____
3. _____
4. _____
5. _____

I would like to learn more about the following *realistic* activities:

1. _____
2. _____
3. _____
4. _____
5. _____

Investigative

Curiosity and wondering what makes various things work is an integral part of this category. Most scientific interests fall here. Some examples are doing a chemistry experiment, solving a mathematics problem, reading about plant nutrition, taking a biology course, and studying other special subjects on your own.

I can do and like doing the following *investigative* activities:

1. _____
2. _____
3. _____
4. _____
5. _____

I would like to learn more about the following *investigative* activities:

1. _____
2. _____
3. _____
4. _____
5. _____

Artistic

Many different types of art are included in this category: painting, sculpturing, photography, ceramics, interior decorating, music, drama, creative writing, and creative dancing. Some more specific examples are playing the flute, decorating the living room, doing a still-life painting, and writing a poem.

I can do and like doing the following *artistic* activities:

1. _____
2. _____
3. _____
4. _____
5. _____

I would like to learn more about the following *artistic* activities:

1. _____
2. _____
3. _____

LOOKING AT MY LIFE—18 (continued)

4. _____

5. _____

Social

This category includes liking to be with people and to interact with them in various ways. Helpfulness to others is often involved in the interaction. Some examples are explaining something to a child, working on a committee, entertaining guests, and listening to someone else's personal problems.

I can do and like doing the following *social* activities:

1. _____
2. _____
3. _____
4. _____
5. _____

I would like to learn more about the following *social* activities:

1. _____
2. _____
3. _____
4. _____
5. _____

Leadership

This last category includes being a leader; that is, being willing and able to make decisions and to take responsibility. It also includes interest and ability in persuading and influencing others. Some examples are supervising others, organizing and planning a charity drive, being president of a community group, and selling ideas or things.

I can do and like doing the following *leadership* activities:

1. _____
2. _____
3. _____
4. _____
5. _____

I would like to learn more about the following *leadership* activities:

1. _____

2. _____

3. _____

4. _____

5. _____

●━●━●━●━●

As you look back over what you have written in each category, do you find there are one or two categories with few listed items and others where you hardly had enough room to write all the things you thought? This is a usual pattern. For instance, Barbara had only a few items listed under realistic and investigative but many listed under social and leadership. She said:

Doing this reconfirmed for me that I am very people-oriented.

This process helps you to pick up more threads of your situation, moving you toward ideas and answers to your decision-making question.

Did some of the terms used to describe the categories sound familiar? Many of the same types of terms were used in the values section. This is a deliberate overlapping. The values you have are often exhibited in your interests and activities, leading to more feelings of satisfaction and pleasure. Are there similarities between your values and your interests?

MY HOPES AND WISHES

Take time in this last exercise to unleash your fondest dreams. The instruction for interests was to dream a little, but here feel free to dream a lot. Forget about all the sensible, practical factors of abilities, money, family responsibilities, and reality. Let your yearnings and your fantasies run free. Include those that may seem wild and far fetched and those that may seem simple and mundane yet important to you. You might find it easier to do this by using the following starting statements.

"If I were richer . . . ."
"If I lived somewhere else . . . ."
"If I were 10 years younger . . . ."
"If I weren't married . . . ."
"If my children were older . . . ."
"If I didn't have children . . . ."

Use whatever method helps you best express your inner hopes and wishes.

•━•━•━•

LOOKING AT MY LIFE—19

- *I Have Always Wanted To Statements*

Complete the following sentences. Remember, do include even the dreams that seem impossible.

I have always wanted to:

1. _____
2. _____
3. _____
4. _____
5. _____

•━•━•━•

Barbara's inner hopes and wishes were:

1. to travel
2. to have more time to read
3. to have more time to do my work
4. to have more education

Dreaming, hoping, and wishing are not idle exercises. They often provide useful information about you. It may be impossible to fulfill your dreams totally, but the hopes may help you formulate ambitions that can lead to practical, realistic plans.

In assessing her background interests, hopes, and dreams, Barbara realized that she really would like to have a degree from a university. However, she still did not know whether she was willing to make the necessary long-term time commitment to achieve that dream.

•━•━•━•

LOOKING AT MY LIFE—20

- *My Learnings*

As a way of crystallizing some of your thoughts that have emerged from this chapter, complete the following:

I learned that I _____

_____

I relearned that I _____

I became aware _____

I was surprised _____

I was pleased _____

I was disappointed _____

I see that I need to _____

_____

I _____

_____

I _____

Five
Where Am I Right Now?

RELATIONSHIPS AND RESPONSIBILITIES

Now that you have assessed your assets and liabilities as an individual person, you need to take a look at your present situation and the people with whom you are involved. Personal relationships are important to women. What others think and feel about what you do and the changes you may make can carry a lot of weight. Also how much other people are willing to change and support you can be a great help or a major hindrance. It will help you to involve the people with whom you live in your discussion and data gathering after you have considered the aspects in this chapter. Check with them about the information you are putting together. Ask them to listen to some of your thoughts, dreams, and new learnings. Ask them to share their impressions, reactions, and ideas with you.

In this chapter you will be assessing your present situation. Later you will be considering the costs, risks, and advantages for you in maintaining the status quo. Also you will be looking at the costs, risks, and advantages involved for you in changing. Taking these things into consideration, you will be able to check out your personal priorities for now and for the future.

One part of this chapter deals with the necessary maintenance tasks of a household and how these are valued and divided among the persons in your living group. This aspect covers the nitty-gritty parts of living alone or with others—from the single woman living alone or with others, to the single parent raising children by herself, to the married career woman, and to the married woman raising a family.

Again, in this chapter there are sections that may not apply to you and your present situation. Briefly skim those

sections. Skimming rather than skipping them altogether may help by raising some questions or concerns you have not considered but which could apply to you. For example, if you are single, thinking of how a husband and/or children would affect the decision you are considering may add useful information to your lifestyle planning. However, concentrate most on the sections that apply to you now.

●━◆━●━◆━●━◆━●

LOOKING AT MY LIFE—21

● *My Personal Involvements*

Fill in and check the blanks.

I am presently:

_____ single

_____ single with a child(ren)

_____ married

_____ married with a child(ren)

WHERE AM I RIGHT NOW?   67

I am living with _____ adult(s) and _____ child(ren).

My Children

I have _____ boy(s), aged _____ and in grade(s) _____

His (their) health is usually
_____ excellent
_____ good
_____ fair
_____ poor

Comment: _____
_____
_____

I have _____ girl(s), aged _____ and in grade(s) _____

Her (their) health is usually

_____ excellent
_____ good
_____ fair
_____ poor

Comment: _____
_____
_____

My child(ren) is (are) involved in the following activities:

_____ sports
_____ music lessons
_____ work
_____ others: _____

in which I now participate by:

_____ driving
_____ coaching
_____ assisting with practice
_____ fund raising
_____ telephoning
_____ committee work
_____ others: _____

This takes about _____ hours per week.

LOOKING AT MY LIFE—21 (continued)

My child(ren) will be at home for another _____ years.

The things I like most about my child(ren) are:

1. _____
2. _____
3. _____

The things I dislike most about my child(ren) are:

1. _____
2. _____
3. _____

The things my child(ren) like(s) most about me are:

1. _____
2. _____
3. _____

The things my child(ren) dislike(s) most about me are:

1. _____
2. _____
3. _____

Do I plan to have more children?

_____ yes

_____ no

My Husband or Living Mate

He works as a (an) _____ and is _____ years old.

His health is usually

_____ excellent
_____ good
_____ fair
_____ poor

If you answered fair or poor, list the reasons and state how this limits his functioning and how it affects you.

1. _____

2. _____

3. _____

His work schedule involves:

_____ regular hours (for example, 9 - 5)
_____ evenings
_____ weekends
_____ out-of-town trips (traveling)
_____ weekly
_____ monthly
_____ occasionally

His salary is $ _____

His salary is sufficient to cover our family expenses?

_____ yes
_____ no

His work involves social obligations in which I participate:

_____ a great deal
_____ some
_____ very little
_____ not at all

He is involved in the following activities:

_____ sports
_____ community
_____ committees
_____ others: _____

I am involved in these activities _____ hours per week.

His style of life is (will be) changing.

_____ yes
_____ no

If yes, the changes I anticipate are:

1. _____
2. _____
3. _____

LOOKING AT MY LIFE—21 (continued)

These changes affect me by:

1. _____
2. _____
3. _____

I feel _____ about these changes.

He believes that women (Finish each sentence.)

can _____
should _____
will in the future _____

He likes me most because:

1. _____
2. _____
3. _____

He dislikes me most because:

1. _____
2. _____
3. _____

I like him most because:

1. _____
2. _____
3. _____

I dislike him most because:

1. _____
2. _____
3. _____

My Relationship with my Husband or Living Mate

In terms of our relationship, I feel:

_____ very satisfied
_____ somewhat satisfied
_____ somewhat dissatisfied

_____ dissatisfied
_____ uncertain

The things I like most about living with someone are:

1. _____
2. _____
3. _____

The things I dislike most about living with someone are:

1. _____
2. _____
3. _____

The things I would like to change about our relationship are:

1. _____
2. _____
3. _____

In 10 years I would like our relationship to be:

1. _____
2. _____
3. _____

Other Responsibilities

In addition to my immediate family I have regular responsibilities to the following people:

1. _____
2. _____
3. _____

These responsibilities are:

1. _____
2. _____
3. _____

They take _____ hours a day/week/month.

I expect that these responsibilities will continue for _____

LOOKING AT MY LIFE—21 (continued)

Possible alternative arrangements might be:

1. _____
2. _____
3. _____

I expect the consequences of these arrangements would be:

Positive   Negative

1. _____   1. _____
2. _____   2. _____
3. _____   3. _____

LOOKING AT MY LIFE—22

- *My Household Tasks*

Most likely you spend a far greater amount of time on household tasks than do other people with whom you live. However, responsibility for household tasks can be shared by others. In assessing where you are, it is useful to examine the physical tasks that are necessary to maintain your home and who does them.

On the following chart, list the tasks that must be completed in your home; for example, cooking meals, making beds, shopping for groceries, cleaning the house, buying clothes, mowing the lawn, and taking out the garbage. In the center column, put down the approximate time each task takes and in the right-hand column write who is responsible for that task.

Some broad task categories have been suggested, but you may need to break these down into finer categories to fit your own situation. You need to be as specific as possible to give a detailed picture of how the tasks are divided within the group. Some people living together share one task such as cooking meals and cleaning up the kitchen. This may be done by taking turns or by doing it cooperatively. In one family the woman may be responsible for all shopping. In another situation a man and woman may share this task, with the woman purchasing groceries and the man buying garden and automotive supplies, or vice versa. In another situation where children are involved, the youngsters share responsibilities by making their lunches and purchasing their own clothes.

Take each member in your household and figure out how much time each spends per week on maintenance. This overview can give you some new insights into the balance of work.

HOUSEHOLD TASKS

Task	Time per Week	Whose Responsibility

LOOKING AT MY LIFE—23

• *My Use of Time*

Household tasks are not the only things that you do with your time, although at times it may seem that way. Use the following chart to categorize your use of time. The daily schedule you completed in Chapter Three will help you remember the many things you do.

TIME USE

Category	Hours per Day	Hours per Week
Household tasks		
Shopping		
Interaction with others		
— Family		
— Friends		
Recreation		
Sleep		
Gardening		
Outside home		
—. Full-time work		
— Part-time work		
— Volunteer work		
— Other		
Time for me		
Other		

Review the Activities List from Chapter Three and these charts on household tasks and time use.

What have you learned:

— about yourself?
— about how much other people help with daily maintenance?
— about the balance of work in your house?
— about how many pleasurable activities exist in your work?

Barbara found this exercise helpful:

The children did not help at all in the house. I was expected to do all things for all people. After completing these charts, I realized what was happening and why. I didn't have any time for myself! I was walking around in a vacuum and getting little satisfaction from my life. Believe me, I started getting a lot more help at home, especially from the children.

Pat, who is single but living with Bill, also found this exercise useful. She said:

When we moved in together, Bill offered to help in whatever way he could. All I needed to do was ask him. This exercise showed me I was taking all the responsibility, and it was hard not to do it all rather than ask for help. As a result, we sat down and decided who will be responsible for which tasks. I no longer need to feel like a sergeant major!

As you review your time use, consider your values. Remember that for the most satisfaction, your values should be visible in your behavior and actions. Review the values you listed in Chapter Three for yourself and your family. How are these values shown in your actions and therefore in your use of time? Are they well reflected there? If so, that is great! If not, can you change your activities and time use to include more behaviors in keeping with your values?

As Barbara began to realize the imbalance of work in her household, she started to teach her children to take on more

responsibility. To her delight and relief, she found they could
be more responsible for themselves than she had assumed. She
said:

My kids are much more independent now! They cook
some of their own meals, they are responsible for cleaning their
own rooms, they have to get their dirty clothes into the laun-
dry, AND they are responsible for doing their homework with-
out reminders from me. If they don't get these things done, it
doesn't bother me. They're the ones who have only dirty
clothes to wear or don't learn what they should from school.
They're the ones who suffer.

I've been really pleased though. The kids are now much
better at organizing their own time. I don't remind them now.
I'm not a nag. They accept responsibility for the consequences
of what they do or don't do.

As you can see, Barbara found this change in workload
very freeing. She felt better about herself for setting limits and
teaching her children important living skills. It also gave her
more time for her own development, a significant gain.

•◄━━•◄━━•◄━━•

LOOKING AT MY LIFE—24

• *Possible Changes in my Time Use*

What changes are possible in your situation?

First, examine what you can change about your own use
of time. Are you efficient in your time usage? Can you coordinate several errands on one trip to make better use of your
time? Can you use more convenience foods or household services to cut down on time you spend on home maintenance? Can
you change your standard of cleaning to be less exact and thus
to use less time? One woman decided to wash her kitchen floor
only twice a week rather than once a day. That freed up about
3 hours a week for her. As you consider answers to these questions and others you may ask, your own values will come into
play. Try to revise your own "I should" messages to "I want
to" ones. Now write your decisions in the space provided.

Some possible changes I can make in how I use my time are:

1. _____
2. _____
3. _____
4. _____
5. _____

Second, examine what you can change by giving some of the tasks to others. Are there any you could request others to do that would help free you and yet not be too hard for those with whom you live, for example, a roommate, your husband, your children? Perhaps you might find, as Barbara did, that the redistribution helps them as well as you.

Some tasks that might be redistributed are:

1. _____
2. _____
3. _____
4. _____
5. _____

You may want to discuss these possibilities with the others in your living group. If so, describe your needs and why you would like some help and relief. You might use your charts as part of the explanation. Then describe in specific, concrete terms what you would like them to do. Try to begin with only a few things, or they will be overwhelmed.

You may meet some resistance. After all, it is quite nice to have someone else do the boring dirty work of home maintenance. However, insist that some change is necessary for you. They may have some alternate suggestions of tasks they would be willing to do and that are more pleasing to them, yet accomplish your goal, too.

As others in your house assume new responsibilities, remember to be patient. Often they are just beginning to learn how to do some of the tasks, so they will not be able to do them as well as you can. They may be slow. And they may not do it to your standard. At that stage it is very tempting to jump in and take over with, "That's OK; I'll just do it myself. I can do it faster, easier, and better than you." This is a trap! Resist those impulses. By taking over you are defeating yourself and telling the others they are incompetent. Be patient. Grit your teeth, if necessary. And reward yourself with the time that is freed for you. Changing your own activities and redistributing tasks are usually not easy. You may need to use the assertiveness chapter to better handle your own guilt feelings and other people's reactions. However, the reward of more personal satisfaction and fulfillment is great.

A thorough assessment of where you are right now is critical to looking at your possible future directions. Only by examining your values, management of time, relationships, and responsibilities, can you clearly see what can develop in your future. The information you have gathered and pondered in this chapter provides a solid base for moving ahead.

●━●━●━●━●

LOOKING AT MY LIFE – 25

● *My Learnings*

Once again, summarize your learnings by completing the following sentences:

I learned that I _____

_____

I relearned that I _____

_____

I became aware _____

_____

I was surprised _____

_____

I was pleased _____

_____

I was disappointed _____

_____

I see that I need to _____

_____

I _____

_____

I _____

_____

•➤•➤•➤•

Six

What Do I Consider
in Changing?

Now that you have assessed who you are, what you have done, and where you are, you need to consider the risks involved in changing or in maintaining the status quo. Continuing your life as it is may, at first glance, seem to contain little risk since that is more of a known quantity. However, even keeping things as they are contains risk and it is in fact a decision, even though it may be a passive one.

Any change, whether consciously decided upon or simply drifted into, involves risk. The amount of risk you can handle well will vary with your situation and your own personality. You will need to consider the many possible effects a change may have on the balance of your current personal situation. Some changes may have a positive effect for both you and others in your life. Other changes might be positive for you and not for others; alternatively, they might be positive for others but not for you. Some concerns and questions for you to consider are raised in this chapter.

Each of us operates in a dynamic network of relationships and activities. When some part of that network or system is altered, the other people involved make adjustments to the change. The adjustment, or accommodation, may be great or very small, depending on how much the person or activity is affected by the change.

For example, Mary decided to take an evening course at the local high school to upgrade her skills. This upgrading would enable her to get a job and add to her husband's marginal income. However, they have two preschool children, and until then Mary had been primarily responsible for child-care arrangements. To attend her classes, Mary had to arrange who would look after the children while she was away. The various possibilities she could consider would affect her social network in differing ways. One solution was for Mary's husband to take care of the children; another was to hire a sitter for the evenings she was out; a third solution was to have her mother come in; a fourth was to take the children to a neighbor. Alternatively, Mary could have made no set arrangement but could try to handle the child-care situation on a weekly basis. There are probably other possibilities, but these illustrate the concept. With each solution to her child-care problem there is a slightly different impact on each person and Mary's relationship to her or him. The solution for her may be a very simple one, or it may be highly complex because of expectations she has about herself or others have of her.

Another example shows how a decision can be beneficial to you but damaging to your relationships with others. Consider when Jane, a single career woman, took on a more responsible position with her company. The new job was very demanding of Jane's time; she no longer worked a neat 9-5 schedule but had after-hours meetings and put in other overtime. Her job also involved traveling, so she was out of town about a week out of every month. Jane was thrilled with her opportunity and threw herself into the work with energy and enthusiasm. However, her relationships with two close friends suffered because she no longer had time for them. She had not foreseen this effect of her new position.

When you are considering a change in your lifestyle, you may face different and potentially more serious ramifications than those Mary faced with her child-care problem or Jane with her friends. The positive and negative consequences need to be thought through as clearly as possible so that you and others can plan well. After considering the consequences, you may decide these changes are not worth the price.

The factors which are raised in this chapter for you to consider in making your decision are based on the types of questions, fears, and thoughts experienced by many women who have already struggled with this process. These concerns are your self-confidence, the way you manage time and organize activities, your energy level, finances, personal satisfaction, and your attitudes and feelings about the role of wife and mother (if applicable). The concerns listed here are not meant to be a complete inventory, and each does not necessarily rule out another. You may find as you explore your own thoughts that you can add to this list, and you will probably find that several of these items may be very intertwined in your own circumstances. Each of these topics will be considered with thoughts and ideas gleaned from many sources. This discussion is not meant to provide answers but to indicate areas of concern other women have had, questions you should raise in your own mind, and some potential solutions.

SELF-CONFIDENCE

You may doubt your own abilities to move from familiar circumstances to a new situation. While you have confidence in some or many areas of your life, you may find other areas where you feel shaky—a pattern which is characteristic of most people.

Many women question their ability to learn, think, speak, and act in ways which will do them credit. For example, Rosa is a "cracker-jack" secretary. Her boss feels that she has skills which could be developed in the company's leadership program. This training would lead to a middle-management position. Rosa is intrigued with the idea but questions whether she would really be able to handle the new skills, learning, and responsibilities. Her doubts and fears have paralyzed her so that she has missed two training opportunities.

Many women who have been primarily mothers and housewives feel quite isolated. Skills once held seem to have become rusty, or perhaps the skills and knowledge were never developed. As Barbara said:

With three children spaced pretty close together, I was so busy I didn't have time to think of myself. I had no confidence in myself at all. When I started thinking of going outside my

home, I was really scared! I couldn't stand it, and if I hadn't got-
ten out from under I would have cracked up. I joined a women's
group out of desperation.

Women are often judged on their homemaking competencies by members of the family, guests, and others who know
how the husbands and children look and behave. However,
there is not a consistent, planned judgment, which means homemaking can be a more private and self-controlled situation than
most other work. This provides freedom that allows a homemaker to set her own standards, work at her own speed, make
her own mistakes, and organize activities to suit her own situation and pace. This freedom is offset by the negative effect of
little and erratic feedback. It is difficult for a woman to know
how well she is performing her work since it is not consistently
evaluated, and she receives no pay raises for improvement or

excellence. Barbara said:

Some of my dissatisfaction at home was that Paul never comments and probably doesn't notice changes and improvements at home. He couldn't even tell you what colors the rooms are! I didn't feel I got much reward or recognition for being at home. But I don't know many women who do. I felt really taken for granted.

The universal method of recognizing worthwhile work is money, and homemaking is not rewarded in this powerful way. Thus the contribution of homemakers is often underestimated or even overlooked when society evaluates productive work.

This down playing the value—or, lack of recognition—by society for homemaking often leads women themselves to devalue, or underrate, their work. "I'm just a housewife" or some similar statement is often made. There is also a tendency to feel that anyone is capable of doing housework, that "If I can do this work, anyone can. So what?" If society devalues what you do and you devalue what you do, it is very difficult to feel positive and self-confident about yourself and your competencies.

Negative thoughts about homemaking or your job also usually mean that you devalue any compliments from your family and friends for a job well done.

Ingrid has just finished redecorating her son's bedroom. She painted the room and made a matching bedspread and drapes. Ingrid thinks the room now looks better but also feels most anyone could have done it; in fact, someone else might have been able to be more creative. Other people did react.

Ingrid's husband: Gee, Joe's room looks really nice. You did a good job, Ingrid.
Ingrid: Do you really think so? It may have made the room a little darker.

Ingrid's son: Wow! Thanks, Mom, I think my room looks great!
Ingrid: Joe, stop bouncing on the bed! You'll really have to take care of your room now and not leave it in such a mess.

Ingrid's friend: Ingrid, Joe's room looks terrific. What a clever way you chose to make the room look larger!
Ingrid: Well, I had a terrible time deciding on colors. Besides, don't look too closely or you'll see all the mistakes I made.

In each instance, Ingrid was unable to accept the praise, and perhaps she did not even hear it. Instead, she responded by questioning her husband's sincerity, drawing attention to mistakes, and calling down her son. The recognition of her work and success was there, but Ingrid, in devaluing herself, missed the praise that she could use to help raise her self-confidence.

While homemakers often express lack of self-confidence and doubt their abilities to function outside the home, women in other circumstances also express doubts. Many women who are working doubt their abilities to take a more responsible position or go back to school to increase skills and change career directions. Although change can be risky, too many women are unnecessarily modest about their capabilities.

You, like all people, need recognition, information, praise, and criticism from others and yourself about your performance in living. This is how you can evaluate your own effectiveness and make adjustments, if necessary, in how you function. You begin to doubt your abilities and skills when this feedback does not occur, when the feedback is overlooked, or when the feedback is not accepted. Remember that you need others' opinions, but you also need confidence in your own opinions of yourself so that you can accept or reject outside judgments appropriately.

There are many reasons why you as a woman may lack self-confidence. Direct and indirect messages from the media, parents, friends, and other people tell you what you should be like. The emphasis is for you to be attractive, socially poised, and helpful to others. There is little emphasis on developing your intellectual, manual, and political skills. Contrasting the position of most women in our society with the visible political and economic power of men may leave you feeling less able than men. To change these forces in society which shape self-concept is a tough, uphill fight. Unfortunately, you may learn to accept society's attitudes, leading you to have low self-esteem.

Being more personally active can help you overcome feelings of low self-esteem. Activity puts more of your behavior out for view and response. From this you can gain information about your impact on other people. You also can practice skills important to getting along well with others.

Finding support from other women in similar circumstances also has been very effective for many women. Admitting the need for such support and seeking out one or more women with whom to share your concerns and from whom you may receive recognition may be your biggest and most vital step to gaining self-confidence. Joining a sorority was Barbara's first step in gaining her self-confidence. In this group she began to get involved in leadership activities and received support from the other women. She commented:

Joining a sorority made me think, because there were women who were single, some who were separated or divorced, and others like me. There were a lot of different points of view that I had never known. I also made a lot of friends doing various things that involved activities outside the home. There was a lot of support from them because they had many of the same feelings as I did. It was really important for me to be able to talk with other women in the same boat.

Lack of self-confidence can make you afraid to put yourself in the public's view where you can and will be judged. Making your skills public means being open to judgment. In turn judgment means running the risks of ridicule, not getting an expected raise, not being elected to the committee, or not making the team. More positively but often as threatening, it means being congratulated, being promoted, being elected chairperson of the committee or captain of the team! Do you fear or welcome such publicity and judgment? Why? If you fear it, what can you do about it? In a later chapter there will be some suggestions about how you can become more assertive and better able to handle the positive and negative situations, which in turn can help you feel greater self-worth and confidence.

TIME MANAGEMENT, ORGANIZATION
AND ENERGY LEVEL

The factors of time management, organization, and energy level will be considered together since they are so closely related. From the time charts you completed in Chapter 3 you have a clear idea of how you now spend your time. You may be saying, "I don't have time to do anything more" or "I spend too much time on X when I'd rather be doing Y" or "I could do a lot more if I would just . . . ." or "I really like my life pretty much as it is for now, but I want to plan for the future."

A common anxiety and concern among women considering a major change is how to organize themselves and their families to make the most effective use of time and effort. Taking an educational program or working can be the most demanding of the choices because there are usually time schedules, deadlines, and perhaps some unpredictable demands made by others, such as homework, unexpected overtime, or practice of new skills.

Most women can do more if they want to or, more importantly, do more of what they really want to do. For you this will mean making some choices and perhaps changing the way you do things. Violet, who did the time scheduling exercise, was quite surprised. She had already been taking university classes for the past 3 years. Violet said: "I did this exercise and discovered that all this time I really have not had time to go to school and take all these credits, let alone study and get good marks. It just goes to show, doesn't it? When I am at school, that is, doing what *I want*, then I simply make time because I operate from a different point of view."

Lois Hoffman and Ivan Nye, two researchers, report that one of the effects of married women working outside the home is a different use of their time.[1] They found that while employed women continue to participate in voluntary community organizations, they work less in the leadership of these organizations compared to nonemployed women. Employed mothers also reported a reduction in the following recreational activities:

TV viewing, daytime neighborhood visiting, formal entertaining, and golf playing. No significant differences were found between employed and nonemployed mothers in spouse- or family-oriented recreation. The results did not indicate whether employed women considered taking fewer responsible positions in community groups or reducing certain recreational activities as a deprivation.

Whatever rearrangement of your own time you may be considering, be careful to sort out which activities you already have that are essential to your well-being and self-esteem and those which are dispensable. If being able to swim regularly is important, you do not want to take on some activity which will interfere. Or if being in charge of organizing the finances for the local political party gives you vital personal recognition, then you do not want to take on additional activities which would not allow you time for this political involvement. These are examples, but they highlight the type of thinking and weighing of alternatives you have to do.

You may wish to review your proposed schedule from Chapter Three and changes you considered in Chapter Five in light of this information. There are two large components in making decisions about time. One is choosing *what you will do* from among all the tasks and alternatives. The other is finding how to be as *efficient* as possible in your use of time. Some suggestions in both of these areas were provided in Chapters Three and Five. You may already be a well-organized person and have developed some techniques of your own to maintain your level of efficiency. Good! Women often are already very efficient but may have to look closely at their time priorities.

Nancy is a highly organized woman whose efficiency was the envy of some of her friends. She claimed her secret was careful planning. Although Nancy's time was more tightly scheduled than would feel comfortable for many people, she insists, "I can handle things better emotionally and get so much more done when I know ahead of time just what I'm doing. I like my life to be predictable, and I arrange most of my time to meet that need."

Obviously, a schedule allows you to get organized and to plan ahead. Planning ahead is a key element, no matter what your specific needs are.

Your energy level can vary with a number of factors: age, physical condition, and emotional demands. Some people are more energetic than others; they seem to move faster, with vigor and definiteness. Others are more slow paced or run out of steam sooner, and they need more sleep and rest. Do you marvel at how much some people accomplish, or are you one at whom others marvel?

Part of accomplishment is organization and skill, and part is how you apply the energy you have. The demands for energy vary from one time to another. When children are young, there is a lot of physical care in lifting, carrying, bathing, dressing, feeding; not to mention the constant watching to keep them from harm. No wonder mothers of young children often feel tired. As children grow older, there are greater verbal and emotional demands which can take less or more energy, depending on you and your reactions to these demands. In today's lifestyles there may be special demands for and by children. Barbara lives on an acreage. Although her three children are not involved in many activities, she does a lot of chauffeuring. She makes about four to six trips a day to town. This adds up to approximately five hundred miles a week and takes time and energy. Another possibility is that your energy demands are seasonal, for example, with more demands in spring and summer when your garden requires special care. In any case, you are your own best judge of how much energy you have and whether the demands on your energy will vary from time to time.

You can increase your energy level by improving your physical condition. People who maintain good physical condition by exercising regularly and eating a nutritionally balanced diet function better emotionally and intellectually. What about you? Would a program to improve your physical condition be an important first step to enlarging your set of activities? Is improving physical condition a part of your program for greater self-fulfillment?

If you want to improve your physical condition, there may

be programs in your community to help you get started, for example, the "Y." If you prefer to work on your own, you might try one of the many self-help books available. Many are available in paperback and provide a range of physical fitness activities that you can adapt to your own schedule and the facilities available to you. You should plan physical fitness activities which you can do regularly over a long time. Physical fitness is a lifetime commitment.

FINANCES

What you can consider for yourself may depend on your financial status. Money is a consideration in most decisions. If you are married, is your husband the breadwinner? Is his salary sufficient for your family's needs? Is there enough for you to take on an activity that may cost money? Do you need to consider earning money? Soon? Or at some time in the future?

If you support yourself, can you afford another budget item? Can you change your priorities? Or are there other sources of monetary support so that you can participate? If you are thinking of taking a course, have you considered all the expenses that might be involved: transportation, clothing, equipment, materials, fees, books, as well as any new expenses for child care, housekeeping, or increased food bills for convenience foods?

To avoid embarrassment or resentments later, be sure to work out the economics of your plan well in advance. This may mean sitting down with your own or the family budget and getting a clearer picture of where the money goes, what the current priorities are, and what the expected future ones will be.

Another aspect of this picture is whether financial pressures are forcing you to earn money or more money than you now do. If you think that additional income is necessary, you may be considering employment, training, or retraining for a future career. Pressure may also come from expected changes in your marital and financial status, for example, a trial separation, or from wanting to be prepared for unexpected changes, for example, your husband's illness.

PERSONAL SATISFACTION

This is a less specific area to discuss because to obtain personal satisfaction requires the most unique solutions. Basically, personal satisfaction is a feeling about yourself and the way you are living your life—that you are achieving what you want to for *you*. What you want for yourself may include helping others, usually family and friends, to accomplish their goals. But, as has been emphasized before, women tend to be "other-directed," meeting the needs and demands of others while denying their own needs. Often the result is that women do not even know what their needs are. They give their needs too little attention and priority. Margaret Adams, a social worker, has expanded on this theme, which she calls the "compassion trap":

> The main target of my concern is the pervasive belief (amounting almost to an article of faith) that woman's primary and most valuable social function is to provide the tender and compassionate components of life, and that, through the exercises of these particular traits, women have set themselves up as the exclusive model for protecting, nurturing, and fostering the growth of others. (p. 556)[2]

Later Ms. Adams extends this notion of the "compassion trap" beyond the family situation to include employment situations as well:

> Both family and professional commitments incorporate the insidious notion that the needs, demands, and difficulties of other people should be woman's major, if not exclusive, concern and that meeting these must take precedence over all other claims. Implicit in the role that derives from this conviction is the virtue of subordinating individual needs to the welfare of others and the personal value and supposed reward of deriving a vicarious satisfaction from this exercise. This *indirect* expression of talents and skills and these rewards reaped second-hand are probably the chief feature distinguishing women from men in their professional lives. (p. 559)[3]

These are strong statements, and you may not think they

apply to you, or you may immediately identify yourself as being caught in the "compassion trap." Getting out of this trap does not mean that you are no longer sensitive to the feelings of other people. It does mean that you value your own feelings and respond to them with the same sensitivity and attention you give others' feelings. Maintaining a balance between your own needs and wants and those of other people who are significant to you is important for your personal feelings of confidence and fulfillment. Barbara is well aware of these statements and their importance. However, she still describes herself in this way:

I'm always crawling out of the compassion trap! One of the best ways for me to get out of that trap is to physically just not be present.

If you recognize that you are in the compassion trap, you may want to consider becoming more assertive, which is discussed in Chapter Eight.

Another related but different angle on this issue of personal satisfaction is more specifically related to male-female relationships. Many women are in marriages or other relationships, for example, parent-child, employer-employee, in which there is an unequal power balance in terms of emotional demands. Richard Stuart calls this the power balance of "I love yous."[4] Everyone has various sources of support and love, and each person usually returns some or equal support and love to the sources. Thus these are reciprocal relationships. When a relationship is out of balance, a person is usually giving more emotionally than he or she is getting in return, or vice versa. This imbalance may be all right in some relationships, as with certain stages of childhood when parents invest more in the child emotionally than is apparently being returned. An equal return on this investment is not expected or demanded. Or in some intimate or friendship situations a person may give or take more at one time than another because one person's needs are greater. However, overall the underlying expectation is for a balance of emotional output and input.

Stuart represents this emotional situation by showing the sources from and to which husband and wife receive and give their "I love yous." As an example, Liza may receive 25% of her support and love from her children, 20% from friends and relatives, and 5% from recognition for her work on the Home and School Executive (P.T.A.). The remaining 50% needs to come from her husband, Kurt. What are Kurt's sources? Kurt may need to receive "I love yous" in the following balance: 15% from his children, 25% from his wife, 5% from friends and relatives, and 5% from community involvements. The other 50% comes from his work situation. These percentages are hypothetical since emotional needs cannot really be measured accurately in this way, but this example shows how someone can be "socially bankrupt," to use Stuart's term, when there is an uneven give and take in a love relationship. Liza needs more from Kurt than he needs from her or gives to her. Kurt's work occupies a good share of his time and emotional energy outside the home and the family relationships. His work is a compelling interest, an essential part of his identity. In this situation Liza can feel dissatisfied and unfulfilled. The imbalance in emotional exchange is an important cause for the lack of personal satisfaction Liza and many women experience in relationships.

Most people enter and continue an intimate relationship expecting a more or less equal emotional balance. This balance may exist for a time in the beginning and sometimes may continue. Typically the wife's investment in the marriage relationship is or becomes greater than the husband's.[5] Her focus is in the home and in maintaining social relationships while his is at work as well as at home.

This model may or may not apply to your own circumstances, and perhaps not in the extreme presented here. If the example of Kurt and Liza's relationship does seem familiar or puts your situation into a different focus of understanding, you may comprehend your lack of and need for personal satisfaction in a new way. Your current relationships may not be adequate to completely fulfill your needs. You may need more challenge and meaning—something that is an achievement of your *own,* an expression of *your* identity.

THE WIFE/MOTHER ROLES

When people live together in marriage or in another type of ongoing relationship, certain patterns of behavior and expectations develop in the relationship. Often these expectations are just assumed, and it is only when some disruption occurs that a person becomes aware of the assumptions being made about what her or his partner will do, what her or his attitudes are, and what she or he feels. This is part of the "taking it for granted" syndrome in which people move along in life without examining or questioning their relationships. Although constant examining of a relationship can be tiresome, some understanding of it is necessary to avoid shocks and disappointments. A situation can be shattering if one person makes a sudden announcement of a new plan in a relationship.

Many women who decide to change have received active support and encouragement from husbands and children. Indeed, some women originally get the idea to change from their families and may have to overcome some of their *own* resistances before doing something new.

However, some women do find that just the fact that they are actively thinking about their lives can cause great discomfort for those close to them. A man may fear what changes are in store and wonder how they will affect him. One husband flatly told his wife, "You can do anything you want as long as it doesn't affect me!" That is probably impossible. When one person in a relationship begins to grow and change, it inevitably affects the other person. What happened to Barbara is fairly typical:

While I was changing, my relationship with Paul wasn't easy. There were a lot of ups and downs. When I first decided to go back to take some courses, Paul thought that was kind of fun and interesting. It kept me busy and thus happy. However, as I began to change due to the courses, I wanted our relationship to change, to become more intimate. At that stage, Paul decided that the courses I was taking were a bunch of garbage.

When you decide to take a step forward on your own

behalf, you may have to begin without support of those people immediately involved. This action, although difficult, can have a positive effect for you which, in turn, can benefit your relationships. Some husbands and children have been amazed to find that they like such changes and the side-effects. Unmarried women can find that persons close to them may also like such changes. Barbara found:

A lot of good things started to happen. My relationships with my children improved a lot. We were all able to talk about feelings. The kids saw me as an individual with needs, not JUST mother.

Why do some men and children struggle against changes? One reason is fear of change itself and the unknown possible shifts in the balance of their own lives. People get into a familiar, comfortable pattern of living and do not want that balance upset. For instance, Barbara's husband and children really like her homemade bread and cookies. They resisted change that involved Barbara's time being spent on other activities that she found more fulfilling. A related concern is that if you do something more outside the home, you will do less at home (A possibility!). Thus some of the household tasks may shift to them (Also possible!). Sharing the household tasks can have positive effects on all concerned, but that remains an unknown at this stage of decision making.

Some of the concerns of a man are the following: that you will not be available when he wants you to be; that you will become less dependent on him; that you will lose your femininity; that you may associate with other men who are your fellow workers, customers, instructors, students, etc., who could pose a threat to your affection for him; that you will develop intense interests and/or competencies in which he cannot or does not participate; that if you earn money he will lose his economic control over you, and he will have lost part of his identity as the sole breadwinner.

Some or all of these concerns may sound familiar. Possibly

your mate or husband may have none of these reservations. The concerns should be discussed openly so they do not crop up later as issues that separate you. Working out these concerns can lead to better communication about the needs you each have. This, in turn, can lead to more understanding and support for both of you to meet your personal needs in new ways.

For Barbara it worked out:

My children and friends feel positive about the changes I've made. Paul feels I am about the same as ever. However, I feel it is essential to my survival that I continue with my outside activities even though he is not completely convinced yet.

What about your own doubts? A common concern a woman may express when she contemplates change is that her children and husband may discover she is not as vital to their daily well-being as she now thinks and hopes she is. The *need to be needed* is a powerful motive for most people. To fulfill this need it appears that women often try to feel indispensable to their families. Often this is the only aspect of life that makes a woman feel worthwhile. This may be due to society's strong pressures to feel fulfilled by having the cleanest oven, the whitest wash, the showcase home, the most nutritious meals, etc. The tasks assume great importance, but the feelings of love and caring may somehow get lost!

It is possible to have two sets of very conflicting feelings in this area. On the one hand, you may want to be more independent of your family so that you can do things that are personally fulfilling. However, at the same time, you may want them to be as dependent as ever to prove that you are needed. It is difficult to resolve this conflict. The key for many women has been to realize that they as individuals do have some personal rights and that their families care for them as persons rather than as personal slaves and doormats. If you too can realize that your family loves you apart from their need for you, perhaps you can see the tasks you do for them in a different light. You can stop using these tasks as the main proof that you are valued.

A related concern, or perhaps effect, is the guilt over possibly neglecting any aspect of the homemaker-mother roles. From childhood, women have been taught that it is essential for them to fulfill these roles. Barbara felt a great amount of guilt when she joined a sorority which took up one night a month. She said:

I had never gone anywhere or done anything without Paul. It felt like it was the wrong thing to be doing. I felt really guilty taking time for myself.

Guilt over neglecting child care is a common concern. Despite much recent research which shows that adequate substitute care is the crux of the matter, women suffer from guilt about potentially neglecting their parental duty. Research indicates that children usually benefit from being in good alternative care situations.[6] Nevertheless, individual women have to come to terms with their sense of guilt and seek the child care arrangement that suits them and their children best. Having good information about the results of studies on the effects of different child-care arrangements is essential.

Employment is probably the activity which would take you out of your home on the most regular basis. The effects of mothers' employment on children, the working mother, and the marital relationship have been extensively studied. The most complete review of this information is in a book by Hoffman and Nye, *Working Mothers.*[7] To oversimplify the situation, their findings are generally positive. Mother, children, and the marital relationship can benefit from the mother working outside the home. You may wish to read the book for a more detailed description of the research that has been done and the outcomes. Hoffman and Nye caution that their review of research findings (mostly based on studies in the U.S. but referring to studies in many other countries, including Canada) should not be used for making personal decisions because the effects on any unique situation may not be the same as the averages on which the research findings are based. This caution is important to remember in your individual decision making.

However, these research findings are to be taken seriously and should lay to rest some of the myths that have grown up about the negative effects of a working mother on the development of her children. The idea that women being away from their children harms the youngsters has been widespread. Everyone has witnessed or heard stories about situations which support these ideas of negative outcome—particularly of children left unsupervised. Granted, there are unfortunate individual situations, but there also are many arrangements which work well for all members of the family.

Examine your own sense of guilt, why you feel such guilt, and what your options are to provide good alternative care for your children and alternative arrangements for managing household chores. Barbara began to handle her feelings of guilt by talking with other women. She said:

They didn't seem to feel very guilty over possibly neglecting their husbands, children, and homes. As I began to go out and spend time on myself, I began to feel much better. So I decided that what I was doing just couldn't be so bad.

LOOKING AT MY LIFE—26

● *My Learnings*

In this chapter, the focus has been on questions you need to ask yourself about your sense of self-worth and confidence, your time management, organization, energy level, finances, personal satisfaction, and your ideas and feelings about the roles of wife and mother. To help integrate what you have learned, complete the following sentences:

I learned that I _____

I relearned that I _____

I became aware _____

I was surprised _____

LOOKING AT MY LIFE—26 (continued)

I was pleased _____

_____

I was disappointed _____

_____

I see that I need to _____

_____

I _____

_____

I _____

_____

•▬•▬•▬•

SUGGESTED READING

Cooper, Mildred, & Cooper, Kenneth H. *Aerobics for women.* New York: Bantam Books, 1972.

Through a point system, this fitness program lets you know how much and what kind of exercise you get by walking, stair climbing, housekeeping, or bicycling. It teaches you to test yourself, figure out how much activity you need, how to choose your plan, and how to measure your progress.

Hilliard, Marian. *Women and fatigue.* Toronto: Ram Books, 1975.

In answer to countless requests, Dr. Hilliard wrote this book to show women, step by step, how to conquer fatigue. She sees fatigue as a woman's greatest enemy. The book reviews fatigue in adolescence, pregnancy, menopause, and middle age, and it deals with the special problems of the career woman, young wife, and hard-pressed mother. Dr. Hilliard also offers ideas to help you release new sources of vitality.

Morehouse, Lawrence E., & Gross, Leonard. *Maximum performance.* New York: Simon & Schuster, 1977.

Each person has the potential to do better at tasks. This book shows you how to achieve maximum performance in many aspects of life. It covers topics like: stop trying so hard, optimal anxiety, dynamic relaxation, maximizing energy, rapid learning, and some chapters specific to sports. The book outlines procedures that can teach you how to make the most of your inner capabilities.

Tennov, Dorothy. *Super self: a woman's guide to self-management.* New York: Funk & Wagnalls, 1977.

This self-management book helps you assess and restructure your life so that you can do what you most like to do, what will make your life easier, more enjoyable, more satisfying. It teaches you to identify your own behavior patterns and how to change them to suit your needs. You can discover what your top-level capabilities are, when they occur, and how to arrange your schedule to fit your potential.

Seven
What Are My Alternatives?

OPENNESS TO OPTIONS

In the previous chapters you have considered many aspects of yourself as a person and yourself in your present lifestyle. Some of the information is old, some of it may be new, some of it may now be reorganized in a different light.

LOOKING AT MY LIFE—27

- *Possible Alternatives*

Keeping this wealth of information in mind, what alternatives are you considering? In answering that question, try to think of all the possible things you might like to do. Some might be daydreams; others might be ideas remembered from your childhood. It is important to forget for a while your immediate judgment of your thoughts and dreams. Try to override thoughts such as, "That's silly!" "I can't possibly do that," "Who me?" These types of thoughts curtail creativity.

Right now list all the possibilities in the space provided. Just write the alternatives as quickly as possible, leaving the thoughts of feasibility until later.

The alternatives I have thought or dreamed of are:

1. _____
2. _____
3. _____
4. _____
5. _____
6. _____
7. _____

LOOKING AT MY LIFE—27 (continued)

8. _____
9. _____
10. _____

•━•━•━•━•

   Obviously, some of these ideas will continue to be dreams and fantasies. However, in this list there may be some germ of a goal that you can realize with thought and effort. The alternatives you have listed may become narrowed when you consider your present and expected responsibilities. Or perhaps the alternatives are so positive that you may need to consider your priorities and rank order the possibilities.

   Consider the information in this chapter concerning the major options most women have before you cast all cares to the wind and take up your heart's desire, before you manage to cancel out all your alternatives, or in case your list of alternatives was short. The advantages and disadvantages of each option will be considered. From your knowledge of yourself and your circumstances you can add to each option aspects that are unique to you. The options that will be presented are:

1. creative and recreational activities
2. voluntarism
3. training or education
4. part-time work
5. full-time work
6. homemaking

Most of these options can occupy your time on a scale from an hour or two per month to many hours per week. It is also important to remember that choosing one option may not keep you from choosing others as well. Your unique lifestyle may be some combination of two or more options, or you may find the options can be accomplished one after the other. For example, a woman who has young children may decide to devote most of her time to their care. While they are young, she may take a few courses which prepare her for part-time work. Later, as her children grow up and leave home, she may work full time.

Another woman may work for several years after she marries. When her first child is born, she stops working for a while. Then the family needs money for a downpayment on a house. So she returns to the work force until the second child is born. When the second child is three, she and her husband are divorced, and once again she goes back to work to support herself.

On the average, North American women work outside the home for many years of their lives. The number of years a woman spends in the work force varies with a number of characteristics, such as marital status and number and ages of her children. A married woman with children will work an average of 20 to 30 years outside the home, and married women without children will work 35 years. Widowed or divorced women will work more than 40 years, while single women work more than 45 years.[1] Knowing these facts, many women decide to prepare themselves for work they would find meaningful.

Many women experience several of these options as their lives unfold. Sometimes the option is one they drift into; other times they have consciously planned for the sequence to develop.

Barbara has found that the process of deciding is a long and searching evolution. One development and one decision evolves, or moves, into the next, and so on. But a thought keeps hovering in her mind:

I'm going to grow up soon, and I need to know what I am going to be.

In fact, though Barbara recognizes the evolutionary quality of decision making and is willing to accept that, she may find she is always in process rather than at some static end-place. This usually makes for a fuller, richer, more interesting life.

Keeping your list of alternatives in mind, consider each option to see if you can add to or subtract from your list.

Creative and Recreational Activities

This category includes all areas of domestic arts, visual

arts, crafts, handiwork, sports, physical fitness programs, yoga, special interest courses, and so on. Many women combine this type of activity with homemaking. You may have developed some interests already but have new areas you would like to explore or expand.

The advantages of creative and recreational activities are numerous. These activities:

— are usually done by choice, so they fit individual interests.
— are usually fun and provide a chance to work with others as well as work alone, for example, taking a painting class but also painting on your own.
— are very adaptive to the schedule of a homemaker and mother or a career woman.
— are consistent with traditional ideas of what a wife and mother "should" do.
— are usually involved with some skill development which is gratifying.
— may increase physical fitness.
— may or may not involve a long-term commitment.

Commitment can be an advantage or disadvantage. You may want to develop and use a skill over a long time, or you may prefer a series of short-term commitments.

Disadvantages of participating in creative and recreational activities are relatively few. Some women state that they are unable to feel enough commitment or involvement in these activities for personal satisfaction. This may be the case for you. If so, creative and recreational activities can be only a partial solution. Costs of some activities may keep you from choosing them. Activity choices may be limited, particularly outside urban areas or in some geographical locations. For example, you might like to learn sailing but have no body of water close by or live where no instruction is provided. Although this can be disappointing for specific activities, hopefully there are some attractive alternatives for you.

Information about these activities is probably available in

your community from educational institutions, school boards, junior colleges, universities, YMCAs, YWCAs, museums, and art galleries. It also may appear in local newspapers and/or magazines. You can teach yourself many creative and recreational skills from books, and you can learn informally from friends.

Voluntarism

Women have a long history of volunteering for various types of service, usually in social service areas. Volunteer work has been seen as an extension of the caring mother role, and it follows the tradition that women provide service to those who are disadvantaged. When the roles of women were more rigidly defined than they are now, volunteer work provided a socially acceptable outlet for women's unused energy.

Many women give free time and labor to various projects on an occasional basis. This may involve working for a neighborhood fund-raising drive, organizing a school meeting, or passing out leaflets for a political campaign. These are temporary, short-term commitments.

When women consider volunteer work as an alternative lifestyle, they are usually thinking about a more extensive commitment in both time and personal effort. Most commonly, volunteer work is not a full-time lifestyle but fits with other options such as being a homemaker or career woman. This type of volunteer involvement is what is considered here when discussing the advantages and disadvantages.

Most women feel strongly positive or negative about volunteer work, depending largely on their own experiences. Some have had good experiences, having found a satisfying volunteer position which used their skills, perhaps provided some training, and allowed variety in what was required of them. Others found volunteer jobs boring, lacking involvement, requiring no skill, and providing too little appreciation or recognition. Still other women who have been volunteers want something more fulfilling or different. It was a useful midway step in their development, but now they feel ready for something else. These women often say they have mixed feelings about their volunteering experiences, having found some satisfactions but not enough rewards to want to continue. Women who have not tried volunteer work also indicate some of these doubts. The forms of volunteer work available, of course, vary by community. And there are specific advantages or disadvantages to particular types of volunteer work.

An important reason for doing volunteer work is the desire to do something worthwhile. It is an outlet for the need to accomplish something meaningful, to express concern and dedication to a good cause. Whether it involves leading the community scout troop, serving on the library board of directors, teaching English to new immigrants, organizing a day-care center in the neighborhood, or assisting on a pediatric ward, the work itself has value to the woman doing it. The work expresses her concern for the social values involved and may have some fringe benefits like meeting people with similar interests.

Of practical concern to women is the number and scheduling of hours for volunteer work. Often volunteers can limit their availability. This control over time is not always possible; for example, required meetings may be scheduled at inconvenient times. However, since most volunteers are housewives, the time arrangements most frequently suit their schedules. This control is a major advantage for women who want to avoid fixed hours and rigid schedules set by others.

Many women do work as volunteers that they could not do as paid employees because they lack the qualifications. This may seem like a paradox; however, volunteer and paid workers often do the same or very similar work, but the volunteers would not be hired. Thus a woman could teach, do hospital work, or handle complex accounting for an organization as a volunteer. Often that same woman would not be able to get a paid job doing any of these tasks. From a personal satisfaction point of view, volunteer activities can offer outlets not otherwise available.

A related advantage applies to women who are thinking about going into the labor force but lack confidence and/or skills to get a paying position. A woman in this situation may see volunteer work as a way of easing into the labor market, testing

out or refreshing skills in a work environment with less pressure than a paid position. Employment involves higher risks and the possibility of harsher judgments. Voluntarism also provides an opportunity to ease into making changes in the way you and your family live, particularly in what they expect of you.

One other advantage cited by some married women is that their husbands accept voluntarism quite easily. Many husbands value the contribution to the community that their wives make. This kind of contribution by the wife is less of a threat to some husbands than the wife's paycheck and career commitment would be. The advantages of volunteer work can be significant when the work is well matched to your interests and abilities.

What of the disadvantages then? A complaint often heard is that volunteer work does not require skills or develop new ones. The work can be routine, boring, and sometimes isolated with few, if any, side benefits that can make even dull work bearable. So advantages that are mentioned apply to those volunteer situations involving stimulating tasks requiring some initiative and skill of the worker. Volunteers also comment that their work is not valued; that is, it "doesn't count." This complaint seems to stem from the lack of recognition. The most powerful reward for work in our society is money. Work done for free is frequently devalued almost by definition. While there are various awards and certificates which are given to volunteers, much voluntary work is unsung. Reactions from friends and husbands often emphasize this aspect of voluntarism, either devaluing it as "something to keep the little woman busy" or emphasizing the monetary aspect, "If you're going to do all that work, you might as well get paid!"

Another disadvantage is that volunteer work can cost the volunteer money. This may be for transportation, child care, uniform, equipment, and books. Sometimes these expenses are covered by the organization, so this should be checked out. Most often, however, a woman is not only giving her time but also paying her own expenses.

If the advantages of voluntarism outweigh the disadvantages for you, you will probably want to get information about volunteer opportunities in your community—usually readily available from institutions that use volunteers, such as YWCAs, schools, hospitals, nursing homes, churches, museums, libraries, etc. Your local library and/or newspaper may also provide valuable leads to finding some of the more interesting volunteer positions. Some communities have volunteer bureaus which coordinate the desires and skills of the volunteer with the needs of the community.

Training or Education

As you look ahead to the future, you may see yourself in a career even though you do not now have the qualifications for it. Beginning to obtain courses, a certificate, diploma, or degree may be the long-range plan for you. Or you may be interested in taking courses for your personal development of knowledge or skills without necessarily having a definite program goal or career in mind.

Whatever your reason for considering a general-interest, technical, vocational, or academic program, one early decision is whether to do it on a full- or part-time basis. While more and more programs are available on a part-time basis, you will still find some in which full-time attendance is preferred or necessary. Most women find part-time attendance is a good way to get back into classroom studies. Not only does this allow them to fit class attendance and preparation into their existing time schedules, for example, other work and family responsibilities, but it is also an excellent way to learn or relearn study skills without the pressure of a full-time program. If you have been away from school for some time, it usually takes a while to become efficient again, or to learn how to learn.

The track record for mature people returning to school is good. Many do find the beginnings are difficult as they learn what is expected of them, how to study, take notes, use the library, write papers, pass exams, organize their time, and train the brain to function effectively. Once this first hurdle is passed, they gain confidence in their abilities as students. Many people eventually take a heavier part-time program or become full-time students. The decision about full- or part-time involvement is up to you and the arrangements you can make at the institution.

The type of program you might take will not be considered here. That decision develops out of your interests and the opportunities available to you. To determine what is readily available in your community, consult with educational institutions in your area. If a program you desire is not available, the counselor(s) may be able to tell you where you can obtain it. Most educational institutions have advisors or counselors to tell you about the various programs offered which might best fit your interests. However, if you are leaning toward going to school, you should be aware of the general pros and cons of further education.

Certainly the advantages are many. If you are working outside the home, you can upgrade your skills so that you can get a better job. If you are at home and considering paid employment, you can prepare for a meaningful and well-paying position. Further training will make you more marketable. Even though many women support themselves and frequently a family, the average salary for females is still much lower than for males. Traditional female occupations pay a lot less than male occupations. For example, a large proportion of women work in clerical positions, which pay less than the managerial positions still most commonly held by men. Even when men and women do essentially the same work, women are often paid less. For these reasons women who anticipate working many years need to prepare themselves to be competitive on the job market. Whether you expect to work from necessity and/or choice, or you just want to be prepared in case something happens, be informed and plan your route wisely.

From the practical point of view, combining homemaking or working with training or academic pursuits is highly feasible. As a part-time student you can take daytime and/or evening classes which fit your schedule of employment and/or family responsibilities and coincide with children's school times.

Since you would be taking courses you choose for your own reasons, you would likely be interested and motivated enough and work hard enough to do a good job. You may find that you have to take some extra courses before you can get into the ones you most want to take. For example, before you can take a university level chemistry course, you may need to take a math refresher course. Or you may have to complete a Grade 10 English course before going into a secretarial program. By planning well in advance you can work out a scheme to complete these prerequisite courses.

While you can schedule courses conveniently for your current lifestyle, you are preparing for the years to come when responsibilities change, for example, when children grow older and leave home. You are developing a breadth and/or depth of interests that provide stimulation and, hopefully, also increase your options for future choices. By preparing now you can explore one or a variety of interests.

Disadvantages of going to school vary more with your own situation. Classes may not be available in your area. If you live where classes are not offered or where the particular subject you might want to study is not provided, you may be able to take a correspondence course. Many people have found that the correspondence courses that are available in many subjects and at several levels of education suit their needs well. Other people work better with classroom structure and stimulation as well as regular help from an instructor.

Some programs are not geared to part-time students but demand a full-time commitment, which keeps many women with families and/or full-time jobs from enrolling. If this is true of the program you choose, you can ask about special considerations or changing the regulations, or you can make some suggestions for creating a more flexible program plan. Depending on your determination and the amount of resistance you meet, you can push your case for a part-time program with greater force. Some women graduating from the Contemporary Woman Program have been able to convince the director of a technical school course to allow them to be half-time rather than full-time students. Their success in the program showed the director that a more flexible policy toward students' course arrangements is workable and desirable.

As already mentioned, many women fear they will not be successful in returning to school. You, too, may feel old and out of touch and sure that you cannot compete with the bright young students straight out of high school. You may also fear being the only "old" person in a classroom full of 20-year-olds. The facts do not back up these fears. Statistics indicate that many older women and men are returning for further education. This means you will probably find two, four, or even more students your own age or even older in your classes. Research also indicates that older students as a group usually have a higher average in classes when compared with younger, recent high-school graduates.[2] Returning students seem to work harder and to be more motivated, which may account for their higher grade averages.

Another potential disadvantage of education is the uneven demands a course can make on your time. Thus you may be able to fit in required study all right but find when an exam is coming up or a project is due that you have to give much more time to the course than usual. If these unusual study demands occur when you are having problems with your boyfriend, a visit from relatives, added pressure or special responsibilities at work, or when your son needs a homemade knight's costume for the school play, you have a real conflict on your hands. Although careful planning and good study skills can help you handle most emergencies, there can be times when you *must* study, no matter what, because a deadline is here. It will mean putting *your own* needs first. Can you?

Most courses cost money. This expense may be a disadvantage for you if your budget is tight. But in return for your money you get pleasure and satisfaction now and perhaps an advantage in employment later. There are grants, loans, and scholarships available to many students, on the basis of need or ability, or both. These funds are helpful, but they are most often given to full-time students. If you want to be a part-time student, you will find that funds are not as easy to obtain. The situation is changing, so inquire carefully. This is not to say it is impossible to get financial aid for your further education, but it may be more difficult as a part-time than as a full-time student. Also the regulations in some places work against the married woman whose husband must show need for a loan based on his income.

Part-Time Employment

Working outside the home on a part-time basis can be an ideal answer for many women who want to do something in addition to homemaking, to supplement other income, or to maintain skills and knowledge. Thus homemakers, widows, and single women who have other income find part-time work attractive. Part-time employment has the advantages of filling extra time, providing less disruption to the rest of your life, and giving you stimulation and social contact. In addition, you can earn money and keep in touch with your occupational field or develop new work skills. You acquire experience which can be invaluable for possible full-time employment in the future. This may sound very attractive to you and may be the way for you to find satisfaction. If you can find a part-time position near your home which fits into your children's school hours, you have the combination many mothers consider most appealing.

As ideal as part-time employment sounds, there are some drawbacks worth considering. The types of positions available on a part-time basis often are not challenging. The work may be boring, routine, and may not contribute to any sharpening of your skills. In many fields you may find it impossible to locate part-time employment so that you can continue in your chosen career. Part-time work outside your field does not keep your skills alive, does not contribute to eventual advancement in the chosen occupation, and is usually not satisfying.

You may find part-time work is an incomplete way to meet your desire to combine family and career. As a part-time worker you may not have the depth of involvement you want in a job. Commitment to work is diluted by the limited time you are involved in the work situation, especially if coworkers are full-time employees so that you miss a lot of work interaction.

Part-time employees do not always enjoy the same benefits as full-time workers, such as eligibility for pension and insurance schemes, paid holiday time, accumulation of seniority, advancement, and job security. A potential monetary disadvantage which you should also explore is the effect of your income on the taxation of your family's income.

On a more personal basis, part-time employment can lead to a married woman's life being overloaded. Typically a woman who works outside the home "only part time" is considered able to carry on with all her usual family-related tasks. While you may have taken the job to fill unused time, the balance may not be perfect. Working part-time can mean putting in full-time hours for part-time pay. Interesting work often enlarges to include more time than was expected by employer and employee. You may find that working requires so much time and energy that you have little left for household tasks. Thus while you wanted to do more, you may find yourself doing *much* more. Of course, a solution is to have the people you live with share the household tasks, but doing this may require that you educate them about your situation, especially if your work has been labeled "just" or "only" part time. Those who have labeled your work this way devalue its importance and can leave you with one and a half jobs! You may have to experiment and do a lot of preparation to develop just the right balance for you. Thus despite its attraction there are some real limitations to part-time employment. Nevertheless, you may be willing to make the necessary compromises and view such work as your best solution.

When you want to work part time and cannot locate a suitable position, you could consider one of the new arrangements now being tried in work situations. Probably one of the most appropriate to consider is joining with a friend who also wants to work part time and who has similar or complementary skills to your own. With good planning you can offer yourselves as a package deal: two people for one full-time job. The two of you can split the work, time, and paycheck on whatever basis suits the two of you and your employer.[3]

You can get information about part-time positions through government and private employment agencies and newspaper ads. Also watch for opportunities that become apparent through newspaper articles. Often the most interesting positions are found through persistent footwork and patience. If you have some ideal position in mind, you may have to search diligently to locate it. The search may take some persuasion on your part, and/or it may take a fair period of time. However, it is surprising how many women have found those great part-time positions no one suspected were there.

Full-Time Employment

More and more women are entering the labor market on a full-time basis. And more and more of these women are married and have children. What used to be a relatively rare and even frowned upon combination—the employed wife and mother—is now becoming commonplace and accepted. Women work to earn money and/or because working is their personal preference for a variety of reasons. With today's rising prices many married women work to help maintain or increase the family's income. Financial necessity is often behind the need to take a job or resume a career. Many women must support families alone because they are widowed, divorced, or separated or because their husbands are unemployed or in ill health.

Often the decision to work is made for a combination of reasons. Women who have to work for economic reasons are usually most satisfied with this lifestyle, if they also *prefer* to work. Many women state that they work because of the excitement and personal growth involved in their positions. For them the money is important but is secondary to other positive aspects of full-time employment.

The advantages of working on a full-time basis outside the home in comparison with part-time work are that you can earn more money, enjoy the fringe benefits offered by your employer, and perhaps have a wider choice of jobs. You can become more involved, have a greater sense of commitment to your work.

Another advantage is that through employment you can return to an activity that may be a very important part of your identity. There are many rewards possible from work: the satisfaction of achievement, recognition by others, social interaction, and intellectual excitement and growth from working with coworkers. These benefits are available to women in full- or part-time positions who are employed in work that they like.

Disadvantages of working full time are largely related to conflicts of time and energy. If you have a family, you inevitably will have less time for home and family demands, yet the demands may not decrease. Thus you can find yourself with two full-time jobs rather than one. How you manage this time pressure depends, of course, on your energy and ability to organize, how you can assign tasks to family members, and what you are willing to drop from your list of activities.

If you are a mother, the ages and health of your children will affect how easy it is for you to work full time. Women with preschool children often find it more difficult to work full time outside the home because child-care facilities are limited, especially for children under 2 years of age. If you can afford and prefer private care for your child, that may be a solution. Such care is usually available, either in your own home or in someone else's home. Lack of good child care continues to be the biggest obstacle to full-time employment of mothers.

You will need to have back-up care for children in case of their illness. This back-up could be provided by someone like your husband (if you are married), a neighbor, or a relative. Otherwise, you may have an understanding with your employer that allows you to stay home during these times. These arrangements need to be carefully worked out since you will want your work time to be as worry free as possible. It is these potential conflicts between your role as wife and/or mother and your role as worker that can be very distressing. There may be times when you simply need to be two places at the same time.

Aside from the time and energy considerations of full-time employment, there are the reality factors: whether there is work available, whether it is the type of work you want, and whether there is the right match between your qualifications and a real position. These are disadvantages only if the labor market is not right for you. Women may find it hard to move, especially if married and if they feel tied to the location of their husband's occupation. Thus you may have a limited area in which to search for a position. If you are a nurse and there is a surplus of nurses in your area, you probably will not look for a position in a distant region where there is a shortage of nurses. Or if you have computer skills which you wish to use but live in a small community where there is no demand for such skills (nor will there likely ever be), you are at a grave disadvantage. This may be no problem for you, but it does pose a serious limitation for many women.

Another reality is the difficulty of finding a well-paying, interesting position. Many jobs which women obtain are routine and do not give them opportunities to use initiative, acquire training, and climb the organizational ladder. These opportunities that are lacking are the very ones many women desire in a career. Overall, women earn less money than men in similar positions. The ugly problems of discrimination are far from over, and you may suffer from them as you search for and work in a paying position. Thus by making the decision to work, you are running the risk of experiencing firsthand discrimination by employers and perhaps others. Discrimination takes many forms, from unfair paychecks to the attitudes people have toward you.

When there is economic uncertainty, women workers tend to suffer greater losses than men. Women's jobs tend to be eliminated first, and because many women workers are in lower positions and have worked a shorter time, they are the first to be laid off or fired. This insecurity as the labor market gets smaller hits women workers the hardest and is a reality which you must take into account as you proceed toward a decision.

You can get information and help in finding a full-time position through government and private employment agencies and newspaper ads. If you are a university graduate, you may be able to use your alma mater's placement organization, and you also may wish to contact Catalyst,* an organization assisting women returning to work. Persistent and patient footwork is often the key to locating your ideal full-time position.

Homemaking

Much has been written about the role of the housewife and mother in today's society. Probably you have been or have thought about being a full-time homemaker, so you can quickly

*Catalyst. 14 East 60th Street, New York, NY 10022.

list the advantages and disadvantages of this style of life for yourself. For most women the homemaking role combines with the other five lifestyle options already outlined. A great deal of how you view this role depends on your own experience, situation, and prospects for the future.

Many women enjoy being homemakers, receiving pleasure and satisfaction from running a smoothly organized household and meeting the needs of their husbands and/or children. While. there continues to be a lot of support for the traditional female role, there are also pressures for a woman to do *more* than be a homemaker or for a woman to consider her future when children will be independent and require much less of her time. Perhaps you are reading this because you want to decide whether homemaking is or will be fulfilling enough for you. Many women have assessed their situations and discovered they really are satisfied being primarily homemakers. They had never before consciously and conscientiously looked at their lives. These women often experience a sense of relief as they realize the satisfactions of their lives, and they can shrug off the pressures that have weighed on them. They become aware that they have made a positive decision to continue as homemakers and are happy with their choice.

The women who decide to continue being primarily homemakers often list the following factors as advantages. A central one is independence: You are your own boss in the homemaker role. Although limited to some extent by the schedules of the family members, you can organize your time and tasks to suit yourself. Depending on whether you have children, the ages of children, appliances you own, your organizational skills, speed of functioning and so on, you may have more or less leeway in how you manage. This flexibility will also depend on how you define your role. Does it include a high standard of housecleaning, lots of home-cooked food, entertaining? Or are you in a less demanding homemaking role? It is important to assess your level of standards, as well as the homemaking itself, since many women lose control over their lives by giving in to external and internal expectations about how they should perform their tasks. The standard can get so high that you can lose control over the work to be done. Only if you have a strong degree of control over what, how much, and when household tasks are done can you consider independence and autonomy advantages of homemaking. Not all women have this control for self- or other-imposed reasons; but it is possible to gain control, set reasonable standards, and make the role more satisfying.

From the media, family, and friends, you are encouraged to continue your homemaking role. Perhaps you are fulfilling your own self-concept, too. This approval from others and yourself is a powerful force which can encourage you to continue as you are.

Providing a comfortable environment for your family and contributing to their progress in school and work is a challenge and can be engrossing and satisfying. Many women are married to men whose careers require a full-time wife and mother at home. These positions are called two-person careers because they require two people to fulfill the obligations of the one paid employment. This situation can occur where a man (it is almost always the man who holds the paying job in the two-person career) works for an organization, is in politics, or has his own business which demands much of his time and/or requires traveling. This type of work may require his wife to be in a social, entertaining, or assistant role. The wife is actively involved in maintaining the husband's career in a variety of ways. Often the wife must maintain the home almost alone if the husband is away a great deal. These demands can fill a woman's life and be satisfying but leave little time and energy for her own pursuits. Another factor is whether this is a temporary or permanent demand, such that you can expect to continue to have your time well occupied or whether the demand will eventually lessen or increase.

Turning to disadvantages of the homemaker role, it is possible to list quickly the common problems of isolation, boredom, repetition of tasks, long hours, and lack of stimulation. Some women find certain aspects of homemaking, such as cooking or child care, very satisfying and find others, such as cleaning, very negative.[4] Homemakers have been found to have more self-related conflicts than women who work part or full time; for example, they may have strong feelings of loneliness, aliena- tion, and/or depression. These concerns have been widely de- scribed and discussed in books and magazine articles, and most homemakers have experienced these disadvantages of working only in the home. Whether you suffer depression and decide to do something else which is meaningful or you feel these dis- advantages are balanced by equal or greater satisfactions as wife and mother is an individual matter.

Barbara's reaction to the alternatives may be helpful:

I feel that I have gone through most of the alternatives at one time or another. I started as a homemaker only. Then I went the craft and bridge route for a few years. Once I joined the sorority and began to move out of the house, I became involved in volunteering. This started with Brownies and Guides (Scouts), the community association activities, and then the city-wide boards. Volunteering met my needs for a little while.

Now I am working part time, so I have stopped some volun- teer activities since I felt overloaded. Part-time work is all I can handle right now because of all the other things I have to do. It gives me a lot of personal satisfaction. However, this way I have time to maintain my home; to maintain my relationships with my husband, children, and friends; and to do volunteer work.

Two drawbacks of part-time work for me are that all the activities add up to more than 100% of the time available and the family feels I should do as much around the house as when I didn't work. I could afford a housekeeper, but I only work part time. So I lay that one on myself as well as getting it from Paul.

As my children grow older, I expect that will free up my time. Then I will probably go to school, which would lead to full-time work. One of the things I have finally realized is that I really like to work.

Some of the advantages and disadvantages of several life- styles have been presented for you to consider. Probably there are other specifics relating to these options which are unique to your own situation, but hopefully this discussion has given you a perspective on these alternatives.

●━●━●━●

LOOKING AT MY LIFE—28

- *A Closer Look at Possible Alternatives*

At this point review each of the alternatives that you are seriously considering and list the advantages and disadvantages of each for you in the space provided. Consider also various combinations of these alternatives, such as being a homemaker, working part time, and having a creative or recreational outlet as well. Listing these points for yourself is a vital step in decision making, so be thorough in your analysis. Space is provided for five alternatives. You may have fewer or more than five to consider.

1. Alternative: _____

   Advantages: Disadvantages:

   1. _____   1. _____
   2. _____   2. _____
   3. _____   3. _____
   4. _____   4. _____

2. Alternative: _____

   Advantages: Disadvantages:

   1. _____   1. _____
   2. _____   2. _____
   3. _____   3. _____
   4. _____   4. _____

3. Alternative: _____

   Advantages: Disadvantages:

   1. _____   1. _____
   2. _____   2. _____
   3. _____   3. _____
   4. _____   4. _____

LOOKING AT MY LIFE—28 (continued)

4. Alternative: _____

   Advantages: Disadvantages:

1. _____   1. _____
2. _____   2. _____
3. _____   3. _____
4. _____   4. _____

5. Alternative: _____

   Advantages: Disadvantages:

1. _____   1. _____
2. _____   2. _____
3. _____   3. _____
4. _____   4. _____

LOOKING AT MY LIFE—29

• *My Learnings*

The summary exercise is provided again since this chapter presents a variety of information which may have generated some new thoughts for you personally.

I learned that I _____

_____

I relearned that I _____

_____

I became aware _____

_____

I was surprised _____

_____

I was pleased _____

_____

I was disappointed _____

_____

I see that I need to _____

_____

I _____

_____

I _____

_____

SUGGESTED READING

Most books listed are concerned with working full or part time. This reflects what is readily available in the present market. To our knowledge, the other options presented in this chapter have not been adequately presented in book form. However, much information in the books listed is beneficial for the volunteer worker and the homemaker.

Abarbanel, Karin, & Siegel, Gonnie M. *Woman's work book.* New York: Warner Books, 1975.

This is a compact, well-researched resource book that describes how to plan and launch a job campaign, how to land a job, and how to know your job rights. The book contains many not-so-obvious points concerning employment; it is practical.

Bostwick, Burdette E. *Finding the job you've always wanted.* New York: John Wiley & Sons, 1977.

This is a guidebook to make sure you are well prepared and well informed to get the right job for you. In addition the book discusses career planning, stresses the importance of exploring lifestyle preferences, and discusses the corporate mind and its relation to job seekers.

Curtis, Jean. *Working mothers.* New York: Doubleday, 1976.

In this book working mothers, their husbands, and children talk about the difficulties they face, the satisfactions they have found, and the ways they cope. Sensible suggestions for equalizing family tasks are made. The emphasis is on the need for compromise and a sense of humor as each family works out its own way of equalizing the burdens and rewards.

Fader, Shirley S. *From kitchen to career.* New York: Stein and Day, 1977.

Shirley Fader challenges the idea that a housewife has lost several years from the job market and thus must settle for a low-level, routine job. She feels your years of living have prepared you for a well-paying, prestigious, interesting job in administrative, office, professional, executive, and business careers. She focuses on real-life experiences of successful women with emphasis on how each managed to survive and succeed during the frightening beginning days.

Hoffman, Lois W., & Nye, F. Ivan. *Working mothers: an evaluative review of the consequences for wife, husband, and child.* San Francisco: Jossey-Bass, 1974.

Hoffman and Nye pull together research findings on the issue of mothers working. They survey the existing data on the motivations leading mothers to find work outside the home; the extent to which women stay in the labor force once they enter it; the relationship between employment, fertility, and population control; the availability and effects of various day-care services; and the consequences of the mother's employment for each member of the family.

Holmstrom, Linda L. *The two-career family.* Cambridge, MA: Schenkman Publishing Co., 1972.

The principles of equality may at times be difficult to put into practice in a family where both the man and the woman are committed to serious professions. This book explores some of the difficulties by looking at real situations in which married couples attempt to work out their own satisfying balance between professional ambition and family relationships.

Lenz, Elinor, & Shaevitz, Marjorie H. *So you want to go back to school: facing the realities of re-entry.* New York: McGraw-Hill, 1977.

This book is for adults who are entering or re-entering the college scene. It gives information, insights, and practical how-to guidance on a wide range of topics: how to study for entrance exams, how to study and make grades, and how to care and handle personal relationships while you get your education.

Loring, Rosalind K., & Otto, Herbert A. *New life options: the working woman's resource book.* New York: McGraw-Hill, 1976.

This guide examines all aspects of your life as a working woman and highlights the many choices available to you today as you face major life changes and consider new lifestyles. The book focuses on five critical aspects:

— new perspectives—approaches for successfully balancing home and career
— getting the best from your career

SUGGESTED READING (continued)

— taking good care of yourself
— the potential of your relationships; living alone, with a man, with children
— managing your options through assertiveness, education, legal rights, management skills, retirement planning

Pincus, Cynthia S. *Double duties: an action plan for the working wife.* New York: Chatham Square Press, 1978.

This book deals with the demands and realities of being a good wife and mother while at the same time benefiting from the experience of working outside the home. The practical nuts-and-bolts of doing both are outlined.

Pogrebin, Letty C. *Getting yours: how to make the system work for the working woman.* New York: David McKay, 1975.

This is an informative guide to the working world. The author shows you how to recognize and overcome the pitfalls and inequities of employment. She also suggests ideas for managing the changes that your working can cause within the family.

Rapoport, Rhona, & Rapoport, Robert. *Dual career families.* Baltimore, MD: Penguin Books, 1971.

This book reports on five families in detail. The couples in the book are: a sales manager and a scientist; two architects who have their own practice; an architect and a TV producer; two senior civil servants; a business executive and a dress designer. All have children. The book examines relationships between the husband and his work, the wife and her work, the two as a couple, and other relationships within the family group.

Schwartz, Felice N., Schifter, Margaret H., & Gillotti, Susan S. *How to go to work when your husband is against it, your children aren't old enough, and there's nothing you can do anyhow.* New York: Simon & Schuster, 1972.

This book attempts to cover everything to help you make a smooth re-entry into part-time employment in a meaningful, challenging job with responsibilities. It is primarily aimed at the woman with a college education.

Scott, Niki. *The working women: a handbook.* Kansas City, KS:
Universal Press Syndicate, 1977.

This book is a series of brief, true stories that illustrate how working
women are coping with their problems. It will help you realize that you
are not alone—that other women, both married and single, share many of
the same joys, frustrations, conflicts, and difficulties about working.

Eight
Assertiveness: Am I
In Charge of My Life?

REACTIONS AND EXPRESSIONS OF FEELINGS

This chapter is designed to help you answer the question, Am I in charge of my life? If your answer is no, the chapter provides some steps that will help change the no to yes. If your answer is yes, you may nevertheless find some new ideas here.

•━━•━━•━━•

LOOKING AT MY LIFE—30

- *Am I Assertive?*

In order to decide whether or not you are in charge of your life, answer the questions in the Assertiveness Check-List. There are three sections: The first lists general situations; the second, specific situations involving acquaintances and others casually encountered; and the third, situations involving close friends and family members. Check (√) those situations that you are able to do at least 60% of the time; place an X where you respond no.

For example, the first question is: "Do I express my ideas and feelings in most situations?" This is followed by a chart for you to indicate whether you do this behavior in relation to one or more categories of people. The responses for two different women are shown as examples.

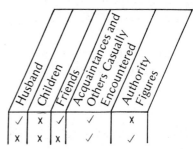

Carmelita answers like this

Marlene answers like this

131

LOOKING AT MY LIFE—30 (continued)

As you can see, Carmelita is able to express her feelings to people she feels close to: her husband, her friends, and her acquaintances. However, it is difficult for her to express feelings to her children and to authority figures, such as a policeman. On the other hand, Marlene finds it easier to express her feelings to people she meets and sees occasionally, like casual acquaintances, the supermarket checker, and authority figures. It is hard for her to tell her husband, children, or friends how she feels.

Go ahead and complete the exercise for yourself.

ASSERTIVENESS CHECK-LIST

	Husband or Mate	Children	Friends	Acquaintances and Others Casually Encountered	Authority Figures	Total Number of Checks
General situations:						
1. Do I express my ideas and feelings in most situations?						
2. Am I able to ask for small favors or help?						
3. If a person has borrowed something of value and has not returned it, do I request that it be returned?						
4. Am I able to feel good and respond with a thank you when someone compliments me?						
5. Am I able to say no to unreasonable requests?						

TOTAL NUMBER OF CHECKS

Specific situations with acquaintances and others casually encountered:

1. Am I able to feel at ease in social situations?
2. If I am disturbed by someone smoking near me, do I request that he or she stop?
3. When a canvasser or salesperson comes to the door and I have no time and do not wish to respond favorably to the pitch, can I firmly but politely say no?
4. If the service I expected in a restaurant, for example, the dressing I ordered on my salad, is not correct, am I able to ask the server to replace it?
5. When I have bought some groceries and discover the milk is sour, am I able to return it and receive either fresh milk or a refund?

TOTAL NUMBER OF CHECKS

Acquaintances and Others Casually Encountered	Authority Figures	Total Number of Checks

LOOKING AT MY LIFE—30 (continued)

	Husband or Mate	Children	Friends	Other Family, e.g., Mother, Brother	Total Number of Checks
Specific situations with family and friends:					
1. When someone asks that I do something for her or him, and I am already badly pressed for time, am I able to say no?					
2. Am I able to request help with specific tasks when I need it (for example, household chores, cleaning up after dinner)?					
3. If people are unknowingly interrupting time I had set aside for myself, am I able to tell them and ask that they respect my time?					
4. Am I able to ask for emotional help or support when I need it?					
5. When someone does something to help or please me, am I able to show my appreciation to that individual?					
TOTAL NUMBER OF CHECKS					

Now add the number of checks you placed on the chart. For each of the three sections, how many checks do you have? Are there more checks in any one section? Are you best able to be assertive with strangers and casual acquaintances? Or are you better able to be assertive with friends and family? Are you able to make requests easily in all sections? Are you able to say no? Are there some situations in which you are able to be more assertive? By answering these questions and reviewing your answers on the chart, try to assess your strengths and weaknesses and write them in the space provided.

I am able to do the following:

1. _____
2. _____
3. _____
4. _____
5. _____

At this point, I find it difficult to do the following:

1. _____
2. _____
3. _____
4. _____
5. _____

In the last responses place a star beside those that you would like to be able to handle more assertively.

You may have discovered that you are able to handle assertively almost all the situations on the chart. If so, you may still wish to read this chapter. By reading it, you may gain some hints on how to handle the situations even a bit better. Another possibility is that you can check to see if you are behaving assertively and not aggressively in handling the people and the situations.

If you answered no to many of the situations, you probably do not feel you are in control of your life as much as you would like. It is important to realize that there are no perfect answers about how you should behave. Also there is no best way you must act in a particular situation.

In assessing her assertiveness, Barbara learned that she needed to be more assertive at home. She was satisfied with how she handled most situations and people outside the family. However, her whole life experience had trained her to do everything for her family and to be "nice." She thought she valued these behaviors in herself. There were certainly no complaints from Paul or the children.

As she became more assertive, Barbara realized that she had been placing her own needs far below those of her family. While her mind consciously accepted these values, her body proved to have been a more accurate barometer of the conflicts between her values and her behavior. She had developed ulcers and suffered painful joint inflammations. Medical examinations showed no physical cause. These symptoms disappeared over time as she began to be more assertive. Barbara believed her physical problems disappeared because she began living more according to her real values which included giving more consideration to her own needs.

IMPORTANCE OF CHOICE

Each person must decide what is best for her at that particular moment in that particular situation. However, it is important that you *choose* how to act; that you actively decide on a course of action rather than being manipulated by the circumstances or the people. It appears that all people are nonassertive in some situations; they may feel that being assertive in a particular situation is not worth the necessary energy or it is not important enough. But when being passive or nonreactive results in conflict, anger, and/or frustration, damage is done: most often to you; sometimes, to others. Although this chapter and its examples show how women are not assertive, this is not a purely female problem. Many men as well as women feel that they are not assertive and therefore are not in charge of their lives.

Research[1] is beginning to confirm what some psychologists have theorized[2]—that when people fail to assert themselves, they lose self-esteem. This losing respect for yourself can become a vicious circle, for as your self-esteem goes down, it gets harder to be assertive. The circle has to be broken. Interestingly enough, one of the best ways to interrupt it is to try a small step in assertiveness and be successful. Successful assertion leads to feeling better about yourself and gives a firmer base for trying the next small step in assertion.

For Barbara assertiveness gradually led to positive results.

While I thought I was doing the right thing by taking total care of my family, I really felt very trapped and hemmed in. I felt the pain in my body, though. It was a long and bumpy move to insist that Paul and the kids share tasks at home. I knew I had made real progress when Mark said, "What's happened to you, Mom? You used to be our slave." However, I must admit I am always crawling out of the compassion trap. It takes continued effort to be assertive, but the rewards for me have been fabulous.

When another woman, Alice, had to go on welfare to support herself and three children, she felt a great loss of self-esteem. She was angry and depressed at having to accept welfare because her husband had deserted the family. Gradually she gained a better picture of her situation and saw welfare as a middle step to the financial independence she preferred. Alice quietly inquired about her rights as a welfare recipient and found she was eligible for vocational training. Little by little, she took the steps to choose a course in medical technology, arrange child care, and make plans to take a prerequisite Grade 12 course in biology. It took Alice over a year to gather information, check out her arrangements, and actually begin her program. With each step in asserting her needs and taking charge of moving toward her goal she gained confidence. She spoke firmly, moved with conviction, and gained a more optimistic attitude.

ASSERTION, NONASSERTION, AND AGGRESSION

Before going further, definitions of the terms that are being used are necessary. People often confuse assertion with aggression. Women express the fear that becoming assertive will make them be "pushy, bitchy broads."

Assertion involves standing up for personal rights and expressing thoughts, feelings, and beliefs in direct, honest, and appropriate ways which do not violate another person's right.[3] The key concept in assertion is respect: for oneself as well as for the other person's needs and rights. The goal of assertion is communication which gives and then gets respect. It is based on fair play and leaves room for compromise when the needs and rights of two people conflict. This does not mean you always win or get what you want. That may often be the outcome. However, the goal is to improve communication, to be able to express your thoughts, feelings, and beliefs. The goal is not necessarily to win. Arthur J. Lange and Patricia Jakubowski refer to this as responsible assertion.[4]

A second kind of behavior is passive or nonassertive behavior. Being nonassertive involves "violating one's own rights by failing to express honest feelings, thoughts and beliefs, and consequently permitting others to violate oneself, or expressing one's thoughts and feelings in such an apologetic, diffident, self-effacing manner that others can easily disregard them."[5] Again, the key concept is respect. By being passive you are not respecting your own needs and rights. Possibly you may not be respecting the other person's ability to handle what you say and feel. The goal of being passive is to keep others happy even when you have to go against your own wishes. In other words, you try to appease others, avoiding conflict at almost any cost. Does that sound familiar? The majority of women in our groups recognize this goal as one of the "shoulds" they had been taught from childhood.

A third kind of behavior is aggression. "Aggression involves directly standing up for personal rights and expressing thoughts, feelings, and beliefs in a way which is often dishonest, usually inappropriate, and always violates the rights of the other person."[6] Winning becomes the goal and may mean winning at any cost: humiliating, degrading, belittling, or overpowering other people. The cost of winning, particularly in an intimate relationship, may actually cause both people to lose. Many women feel that to express aggression is to be unfeminine, so they often avoid this type of behavior.

Two variations of direct aggression are more frequently used by women. The first is an indirect way for a woman to get what she wants. She manipulates by using guilt, trickery, seduction, or sarcasm. With these methods, a person can often get what she wants without revealing her own thoughts, feelings, and beliefs. The added payoff is that the other person has to take responsibility, especially if it works out badly. Many times a person goes even farther with this kind of behavior, becoming a first-class martyr.

Cleo was quickly becoming a martyr. Both she and her husband, Mike, worked. Often when she arrived home after work, Mike was sitting reading the paper. Although she was tired and wished she could sit down and relax, too, Cleo would immediately go into the kitchen to make supper. She would slam cupboard doors and bang pots and pans as she prepared the meal. This was to vent her frustration and anger at the situation and to make Mike notice how unfair it was. When the meal was ready, she would call Mike to the table and almost throw the food at him. Mike would know something was wrong and ask if she were angry. Getting well into the martyr role, Cleo would deny any anger, "Of course there's nothing wrong!" By keeping her actual feelings hidden, she could feel righteous about making supper promptly and make Mike feel frustrated because he thinks he has done something wrong but is unable to find out what it is.

The second variation of aggression often used by women is a "Vesuvius" reaction [named after the volcano].[7] Here the woman attempts to be passive, appeases others, and avoids conflict. However while doing this she feels hurt, angry, and frustrated. There is no release for these emotions. Thus the feelings are stored up and gunnysacked. Each situation adds to these stored feelings until finally she blows up, just like a volcano. Often the Vesuvius reaction occurs over a small insignificant event. All the old hurts, angers, and frustrations pour out aggressively. Those who are the targets of the explosion may be amazed: "Where did all this come from?" "What did I do?" Out of their confusion they often react with equal anger and aggression. Usually the feelings and the conflicts do not get handled because they have been spit out but not discussed.

After the Vesuvius reaction, the woman usually feels very guilty. Often she is also confused by her Jekyll-and-Hyde behavior and thinks, "How could a good, feminine person like me have been so angry and spiteful?" She then vows to increase her appeasement efforts. This may work until the buildup of negative feelings becomes too large, the gunnysack bursts, and another Vesuvius results.

Another possibility in the passive and aggressive combination is that the person may turn the hurts, angers, and frustrations against herself, which results in unexplainable depression. Some women in our workshops say that they have not been angry since they were young, for example, 10 or 12 years old. In many cases there was some severe punishment for expressing anger. However, they say they have been seriously depressed for years, often being in the hospital and taking prescriptions to deal with their unexplainable depressions. Not all depression is caused by nonassertive behavior, but it does appear to be a major factor for many women and also may relate to the vicious circle: lack of assertiveness→ lack of self-esteem→ depression→ lack of assertiveness, etc.

To understand these abstract definitions better, study the following situation and various reactions to it. The situation is that you are waiting in a relatively long grocery check-out line. You have been waiting for about 5 minutes, and the line moves slowly. A man in his mid-twenties has just cut in front of you into the line with a basketful of groceries. How would you react? What would you do and say? Some reactions that help clarify the definitions follow.

Passive: Oh, that's OK, I have lots of time.
Direct Aggressive: Who do you think you are? What a rude, inconsiderate whelp! You get to the back of the line.
Indirect Aggressive: (Speaking to the person behind you in line) Well young people these days are certainly inconsiderate. Can you imagine having the gall to cut into a line-up like this?

Assertive: You may not have realized it, but there is a line waiting to check out. Please go to the end of the line rather than breaking into it here.

The woman who stores up her feelings but releases them in a Vesuvius reaction would probably say something similar to the passive person but would then blow up at her children at home because she has had such a difficult day.

STEPS TO ASSERTIVENESS

Becoming more assertive is a process that begins with small steps and continues as new situations confront you. Your awareness and confidence grow as the process continues. The principles are relatively simple and are based on well-founded behavior modification theory and techniques. However, the doing or changing may be more difficult. Some of the major stages will be outlined here, but for more detailed help you may want to read one of the suggested books in the reading list or attend an assertiveness training workshop.

In learning assertiveness, it is most important to start with the easiest rather than the hardest situations and people and to start with small steps. At first this may seem silly, but it is vital. By deciding on small, relatively easy first steps you ensure that you will succeed. That success is most important since it reinforces your effort and makes you eager to try the next step. If you decide to try a larger, harder step and fail, it is very likely you will not try again. It is too discouraging. Remember, nothing succeeds like success.

First Stage: Awareness and Small Beginnings

The first stage consists of two parts: (1) becoming more aware of how you communicate and (2) beginning some of the easier, less threatening assertions.

LOOKING AT MY LIFE—31

- *My Assertion Journal*

To help you develop your awareness, keep a record of your behavior for one week. Use the definitions of assertion,

LOOKING AT MY LIFE—31 (continued)

passivity, and direct and indirect aggression to help make the situations clear in your mind and describe them. Try to be as specific as possible. You can use the journal form on page 146. Some examples of how it was filled in by Barbara are shown in Figure 2 (page 144). Filling out the journal for yourself will help give you some idea of what situations and people you already handle assertively and will help pinpoint those which you want to handle better.

●—●—●—●—●

When you are focusing on your behavior, be sure to pay attention to both your verbal and nonverbal communication. Verbal means the words that you use in your message. For example, you want your husband to discuss plans for going out on Saturday night. Notice the differences in these approaches.

Passive: Uh, dear, excuse me, but I wonder if we, uh, could talk about Saturday night, uh, if you have time.

Aggressive: George, I'm sick and tired of making all the decisions around here. It's about time you stopped being so wishy-washy and did some deciding. We want to have fun on Saturday night. You decide what we're going to do.

Indirect: The weather report is very good for this weekend, especially for Saturday night.

Assertive: George, I feel like going out on Saturday night. Let's talk about it tonight after supper. It shouldn't take more than half an hour, and it should be fun for both of us.

Nonverbal refers to the many other parts of communication which also carry a message. This includes the way you sit or stand, the level of your voice, where you look, the expression on your face, and gestures you use. For example, the nonverbal language that might be accompanying the previous examples would be:

Passive: standing in slumped posture; speaking in low, whining voice; looking at the floor, having sad expression; using few or no gestures

Aggressive: standing straight, one hand on her waist, the other hand raised with a finger out for emphasis, poking him in the chest; speaking in loud, raspy voice; looking straight at him and walking away after she's finished

Indirect: avoiding eye contact; making casual response and then stamping out of the room and slamming the door

Assertive: standing straight; maintaining eye contact; using firm, moderate voice; using some hand gestures and perhaps giving a smile

It is important for the verbal and nonverbal parts of communication to be consistent so that you do not send more than one message. For instance, you may be using assertive words but saying them in a passive manner. Since approximately two-thirds of the message is delivered by nonverbal communication, most people will respond to your mixed message as if you had been passive. Thus it is important to become aware of both your verbal and nonverbal messages. Be sure to keep track of both in your journal.

Figure 2. Barbara's Assertion Journal

Situation and Date	Verbal	Nonverbal	How I Felt	What I Would Like To Have Done	Why I Didn't Do What I Wanted To Do
Sept. 12. Car in for repairs. Not ready at appointed time. Man tells me it will be another hour or so.	"All right, I'll wait."	Tapped my fingers on counter.	Uptight over waste of my time.	Bawled him out. Demanded a car to use while they finished.	Afraid he would get angry back and make me feel like a fool.
Sept. 16. Mary, a good friend, called to ask me to be a fourth at bridge. She was desperate.	"Sure, Mary, just this once I will." When off the phone, I said, "Now why did I say yes? I really don't like playing bridge, especially with that group. They're so competitive."	Screwed up my face. Set phone back on hook hard.	Annoyed with myself. A bit angry at Mary's pressuring me.	Said, "No. I would rather not. I agree you're really stuck for a fourth, but I can't help you."	Mary is a good friend. She would be angry with me. I may want her to do me a favor sometime.

Sept. 17. Mark, my 16-year-old son, asked me to drive him to a football practice. He asked just 10 minutes before we had to leave when I was just beginning supper preparations.	"Oh, all right. I'll take you."	Slammed cupboard doors. Was quiet grouch in the car.	Angry at last minute notice. Angry at being put out, at his inconsiderateness.	Said, "Mark, I need more than 10 minutes, so I would appreciate receiving more notice after this. Will that be possible? Because you are in a bind today, I will drive you there, but unless I get at least 3 hours notice I won't be able to do it again."	There didn't seem to be enough time. It was faster to just do it. Mark has a terrible temper, and I was in no mood for a fight.
Sept. 20. Paul, my husband, left parts of the newspaper all over the couch and the floor. I had already asked that he tidy the paper up after he is finished.	"You just make more work for me. You're worse than the kids. Paul, you're so messy and inconsiderate! Sometimes I wonder why I ever married you!"	With a great self-righteous bustle, tidied up the papers. Muscles at back of neck were tense.	Angry at his seeming inability to help with even little things.	Told him I was angry without name calling, etc.	I was really mad. He won't listen unless I really get emotional.

Adapted from Lynn Z. Bloom, Karen Coburn, and Joan Pearlman. *The New Assertive Woman.* New York: Delacorte Press, 1975, p. 96. The adaptation is repeated in the following blank form (My Assertion Journal).

MY ASSERTION JOURNAL

Situation and Date	Verbal	Nonverbal	How I Felt	What I Would Like To Have Done	Why I Didn't Do What I Wanted To Do

The second part of the first stage is to start by trying some of the easier assertions. In their book, *Asserting Yourself,* Sharon and Gordon Bower list 11 such exercises that are helpful.[8] One exercise which on the surface seems simple, but which has had extremely beneficial effects in our groups, will be described here. Detailed descriptions of other exercises are listed in the same book.

The exercise involves giving and receiving compliments in an assertive way. One way of expressing positive thoughts and feelings is to compliment another person. When a compliment is accepted, the receiver usually feels a positive boost. Unfortunately, people have often been raised to deny the compliment, which in turn makes the complimenter feel foolish or wish she had been quiet. Some of the negative ways people respond to compliments are: "You can't mean me!" "Oh, I like *your* dress, too!" or "You like this old thing; I bought it years ago at a rummage sale and couldn't find anything else to wear today." You are probably familiar with these responses and perhaps can think of others. In the examples the compliment is denied in different ways. Also the receiver often puts herself down in the process of denying the compliment. To reward the complimenter and to feel better about yourself, it is helpful to acknowledge the compliment. A simple thank you stated in a firm, moderate tone may be sufficient. However, you may wish to add more information in your reply, for example, "Thank you, I really like this color, too" or "Thank you, I enjoyed doing it." Stating responses in this manner indicates a healthy self-pride rather than conceit or egotism. You are acknowledging the compliment honestly, not trying to impress or "one-up" others.

In giving compliments, people may unwittingly word the compliment so that the message is negative. Some examples of these negative compliments are: "What a lovely outfit you're wearing. Too bad they didn't have your color." "I can never do anything with my hair, but yours always looks great." "These cookies sure are good. What bakery did you buy them from?" "What a beautiful scarf you're wearing. I didn't know you had such good taste." It is easy to see why the receiver would be hurt, puzzled, and/or angry with these negative compliments. It is important that compliments be sincere, honest, and not double edged. Learning to give and accept compliments assertively is a way to show others that you care about them.

Barbara kept a record of compliments she gave and those she received and the reply she made or the other person made to her. Here is an example of each.

Compliments Barbara Made   *The Person's Reply*
I really like your new hairdo.   Thanks - it's a good change.

Compliments Barbara Received   *Barbara's Reply*
You are responsible for the   Thank you.
success and efficient way
things are going.

LOOKING AT MY LIFE—32

- *My Handling of Compliments*

In learning this skill, you may find it helpful to record the compliments you make with the responses generated as well as the compliments paid to you and your replies. Use the following chart to record information about compliments for one week.

GIVING AND ACCEPTING COMPLIMENTS*

Compliments You Made	*The Person's Reply*
1. _____	1. _____
2. _____	2. _____
3. _____	3. _____
4. _____	4. _____
5. _____	5. _____
6. _____	6. _____
7. _____	7. _____
8. _____	8. _____

*Adapted from Sharon A. Bower and Gordon H. Bower. *Asserting yourself: a practical guide for positive change.* Menlo Park, CA: Addison-Wesley, 1976, p. 74.

Compliments You Received	*Your Reply*
1. _____	1. _____
2. _____	2. _____
3. _____	3. _____
4. _____	4. _____
5. _____	5. _____
6. _____	6. _____
7. _____	7. _____
8. _____	8. _____

How did you fare in keeping track of the compliments you gave and received? Were you able to do both assertively? Was it easier to give compliments rather than to receive them? This is often the case. From keeping track of other people's replies did you learn any new assertive ways of accepting compliments?

With these exercises now completed, you are ready to move on to another stage of learning to be assertive.

Second Stage: Practice

Until now, you have been mostly keeping track of your behavior in a specific manner to help pinpoint situations and people you already handle assertively and those you would like to handle in a different, better manner. In this second stage the steps for beginning to change will be outlined. Suggestions will also be included to ensure that you choose small steps so that you will be successful and be encouraged to continue working on becoming more assertive.

LOOKING AT MY LIFE–33

- *Situations I would Like to Change*

Look back over your journal and the Assertiveness Check-List. Check those situations you would like to be able to handle differently. Now try to put them in order from the easiest to hardest behaviors for you to change.

Remember that easiest is defined here as very minimal. Make sure you list as easiest behaviors those responses you are quite sure you will be able to change quickly. They may seem

LOOKING AT MY LIFE—33 (continued)

so small that you question whether you should even write them
down. Do! These are the best behaviors to start with when you
are beginning to change. Using them almost builds in success, an
extremely important reinforcer.

Easiest   1. _____

           2. _____

           3. _____

           4. _____

           5. _____

           6. _____

           7. _____

Hardest   8. _____

LOOKING AT MY LIFE—34

- *Replay of a Situation*

Keeping in mind what has been said about small steps, take
the easiest situation (first on the list) and think to yourself
about positive ways in which you might have handled the situation to meet the definition of being assertive. Be sure the situation is easy enough for you to handle successfully. Now, in the
space which follows, write down a description of the situation
and then the exact words you would say if you had a chance to
redo the scene in an assertive manner.

Description of the problem situation (Include who was involved,
place and time, what happened, how you felt):

_____

_____

_____

_____

_____

_____

_____

_____

What I would say to handle the situation assertively is:

_____

_____

_____

_____

_____

Now, read over your new written response. Check it for signs of passivity (for example, overapologizing); aggression (for example, name-calling); and passivity-aggression (for example, sarcasm). Do you feel your new response is assertive? Yes? Great! If not, rewrite your response, correcting areas that need improvement.

Rewritten Response:

_____

_____

_____

_____

_____

Bower and Bower refer to writing out the responses as scripting and suggest that each script contain four aspects: description, expression, specification, and positive consequences.[9] In the first step your response *describes* the other person's behavior objectively and exactly. Use simple, concrete, descriptive terms, avoiding the traps of implying the other person's motives and of using absolute phrases like "You always . . . ." and "You never . . . ." For example, "The last three times I have made this stew, I noticed that you have eaten only a few forkfuls" rather than "What's the matter? Don't you like my cooking?"

The second aspect is that the response expresses your feeling about this behavior. It is essential to *express* feeling statements as "I" statements; for example, "I feel frustrated . . . ," "I feel angry . . . ," "I believe that . . . ," or "I think that . . . ." rather than "You" statements; for example, "You make me angry . . . ," "You're insensitive," "You make me feel unloved."

The receiver is likely to think these "You" statements are angry and blaming, and she or he probably will deny them and/or get very angry. The "I" statements are usually better received, and the person is more inclined to listen rather than to react quickly in a negative manner. To carry the previous example further:

Assertive	*Ineffective*
Describe: The last three times I have made this stew, I noticed that you have eaten only a few forkfuls.	What's the matter? Don't you like my cooking?
Express: I feel hurt when you don't seem to like something I cook.	You make me feel like a failure as a wife and mother.

The third aspect *specifies* how you would like to see the behavior changed, keeping in mind that you might need to change your own behavior. It is best to ask for a behavior change at an appropriate time. Do not request a behavior change of someone as he is rushing out the door. It is also important that the request is reasonable and within the power of the person. In response the other person may also ask that you change some aspects of your behavior, which may lead to negotiation. Back to the stew example.

Assertive	*Ineffective*
Specify: If you don't like something I cook, would you please tell me right away.	Say something!

Finally, state what the *positive consequences* will be for the change you requested. The emphasis is placed on the positive, desirable consequences because you are more likely to succeed by dwelling on these rather than the negative consequences for the undesirable behavior. In emphasizing negative outcomes, people often use threats which are not effective because credibility is lost; for example, "I will stop loving you," "I'm going to leave." Now look at the final installment about the stew.

Assertive	Ineffective
Positive Consequences: That way I will know where I stand and I can feel better, knowing what foods you like and dislike. I also can plan menus accordingly.	Since you don't appreciate my food, I'll just stop cooking altogether.

●━●━●━●

LOOKING AT MY LIFE–35

● *A Closer Look at the Replay**

With this new information, look back at your written replay response and divide it into the four parts: describe, express, specify, and consequences.

Describe the behavior in objective terms: _____
_____
_____

Express your feelings or thoughts using "I" statements: _____
_____
_____

Specify the desired behavior change: _____
_____
_____

State the *positive consequences* you will deliver if the other person keeps to the agreement to change: _____
_____
_____

*Adapted from Sharon S. Bower and Gordon H. Bower. *Asserting yourself: a practical guide for positive change.* Menlo Park, CA: Addison-Wesley, 1976, pp. 123-126.

●━●━●━●

LOOKING AT MY LIFE—36

- ● *Practice for a Future Situation**

So far, you have been analyzing and considering changes in a situation which has already occurred. In becoming more assertive, it is important to expect and practice situations before they occur. Keeping in mind your easiest situation, think of a similar situation that might occur within the next week. Now write out your script, making sure you use the four parts: describe, express, specify, and positive consequences.

New Situation Script

Describe the behavior in objective terms: _____

_____

_____

Express your feelings or thoughts using "I" statements: _____

_____

_____

Specify one behavior change you are requesting: _____

_____

_____

State the *positive consequences* you will deliver if the person keeps the agreement to change: _____

_____

_____

Consider possible reactions the other person might have and write out your assertive replies.

The other person's reaction in behavior and words: _____

_____

_____

*Adapted from Sharon S. Bower and Gordon H. Bower. *Asserting yourself: a practical guide for positive change.* Menlo Park, CA: Addison-Wesley, 1976, pp. 123-126.

Your assertive reply: _____

_____

_____

Once you are satisfied with your written responses, try to have a friend role play the situation with you. After describing the situation to your friend, have him or her read your assertive lines while you role play the possible reactions of the other person in your script. Jot down any more assertive counter-replies that may be needed. Now practice the revised script, speaking your part while your friend plays the other person. Go through the scene three or four times this way, relying on the script less and less. Get feedback about your delivery, keeping in mind your verbal and nonverbal messages need to be consistent. If something comes up which you would like to include in your message, add it and rehearse another time. This rehearsal will help you learn your lines and become more comfortable in the situation.

Next you are ready to try it in real life. It may go just as you scripted, or there may be some reactions you had not expected. Try to maintain your assertive statements and replies throughout the situation. As soon as possible afterwards, write down what actually happened, who said what, etc., and evaluate your interaction. What parts did you do well? What parts would you like to have done differently? If there are any of these, rewrite your possible statement remembering the steps: *describe, express, specify,* and *state positive consequences.* If possible, you may wish to have your role-playing friend share in this critiquing process. Often you may be too close to the situation and want to do it perfectly. You may miss the things you did well. These are important. Remember to accept your friend's positive descriptions in an assertive way, not denying them or concentrating only on the wrong things you said or did. This process will help prepare you for the next time the situation occurs. Look for small, step-type improvements.

Once you are handling that situation in a responsible assertive manner, go back to your list of situations and repeat the whole practice process on the second easiest situation. As you

LOOKING AT MY LIFE—36 (continued)

work through each, you will probably begin to feel more in control of yourself and your life. Being assertive will get easier.

•◄●►•◄●►•◄●►•

Third Stage: Reinforcing your New Assertiveness

While practicing your new assertiveness skills and changing your old behaviors, you also need to pay attention to what you are saying to yourself. Your thoughts can support and assist you with your new behaviors or they can undermine your efforts. This example shows some alternative thoughts a woman might be having as she tries to be assertive with her son.

A child of 9 returns home from school to find his mother just beginning to relax with a book. After discussing the happenings of the day, the child says, "Gee, Mom, I'd really like a peanut-butter-and-jelly sandwich."

Reply: Help yourself, Jimmy. I have just started a short relaxing time for myself and would like to read for 30 minutes.
Thought A: I really shouldn't be so selfish. I should be a better mother and make him a sandwich. It wouldn't take very long, and that way the kitchen won't be a mess either.
Thought B: That was an assertive thing to say. I outlined my limits and have guarded my first and probably only relaxing time for today. Besides it will help Jimmy become more independent even if he messes up the kitchen.

A great difference between the two thoughts! The first thought would probably propel Mother into the kitchen. If by chance she continues reading, she will spend at least part of the time feeling guilty. The second thought is a way of rewarding herself. It is not boastful or conceited but describes what she has done in a positive manner. If your thoughts resemble A rather than B, attempt to challenge them with more rational ideas and fewer "shoulds." This technique of challenging and reconstructing your thoughts was originally outlined by Albert Ellis. You may wish to read more about it in either Ellis and Harper's *A New Guide to Rational Living* [10] or Jakubowski and Lange's *The Assertive Option: Your Rights and Responsibilities*. [11]

•◄●►•◄●►•◄●►•

LOOKING AT MY LIFE—37

- *My Personal Rights*

As your behavior becomes more assertive and your thoughts are approving the new behavior, thus reinforcing it, you may find that you are developing some new ideas or beliefs. You may be beginning to believe that "assertion enriches life and ultimately leads to more satisfying personal relationships with people."[12] A second basic belief may develop, namely, that "everyone is entitled to act assertively and to express honest thoughts, feelings, and beliefs."[13] Thus the definition of assertion becomes more incorporated within you. Many women in our groups have found that the second belief can lead to a real breakthrough in their own thinking: "I have the right to have needs and to have these needs be as important as other people's needs." This then leads to being able to ask people (husband, children, friends) to respond to "my needs" and to decide whether "I" will take care of other people's needs. What a freeing belief!

One of Barbara's significant discoveries was that she did not have to continue to take responsibility for everyone else. She said:

It was the most liberating thing in my life. I suddenly realized I did not have to be totally responsible for anyone but me! It was a real weight off my shoulders.

It may be more meaningful for you to consider your rights in a personal way, for example, right to dislike my brother-in-law, right not to laugh at jokes, right to get what I pay for.

These are the rights Barbara developed for herself.

I have the right to:

— express my feelings.
— live by my principles.
— choose my own lifestyle.
— decide when I accept responsibility.
— judge my own behavior.
— make my own decisions.

LOOKING AT MY LIFE—37 (continued)

— get angry with the actions of others.
— express my anger or pleasure with others.

In the space provided list as many personal rights as you can.

My Rights:

1. _____
2. _____
3. _____
4. _____
5. _____
6. _____
7. _____
8. _____
9. _____
10. _____
11. _____
12. _____
13. _____
14. _____
15. _____

It would also be interesting to write out what you feel are the personal rights of other people in your life, for example, your neighbor's rights, your friend's rights, your husband's or mate's rights, your daughter's rights, your son's rights. Are there any similarities between the lists? You may find yourself coming to a general conclusion about people's rights. For more complete coverage of people's rights you may wish to read Jakubowski and Lange's *The Assertive Option: Your Rights and Responsibilities,* already noted.

CONSEQUENCES OF ASSERTIVENESS

There may be both negative and positive consequences for you in becoming more assertive. People around you may not understand the change, and they may be suspicious. Others may really want their relationship with you to remain the same; they may fear change. It is important to realize that one person's change in a relationship system affects the whole system. For instance, if you change from being passive to being assertive with your husband and children, they are going to be affected individually; also the relationships in the whole family will begin to change. These changes may be very positive for you and your family, but first reactions are likely to be hesitation, fearfulness, uncertainty, and resistance. Be aware that this may happen. Assertive communication about what and why you are changing your behavior can help here.

A second negative consequence that occurs is that as a woman begins to change and tries to be more assertive, a lot of anger and resentment wells up. These feelings which have gone unrecognized may result in her becoming quite aggressive. This may happen to you, too. When you first express emotions after having little or no practice, you may express your feelings in aggressive anger. This is part of a process that often happens when a person tries out new behaviors. In trying for assertive behavior you may overshoot the mark and act aggressively. Consider a pendulum analogy. In finding a balance you may let the pendulum swing from passivity to aggression before discovering the more constructive middle ground of assertion.

Barbara's experience was that as she became more assertive, she overdid it. She remembered:

I don't think I was aggressive in my behavior, but I was unrelentingly assertive! Becoming assertive was such an important new thing in my life that I used it everywhere and in every situation. Particularly with my kids and Paul. They really felt I was pressuring them. If I had it to do over again, I would go a little slower.

A third negative consequence is closely related to the second. As a woman changes from being passive and complacent to becoming more assertive, others may discourage the change by labeling it "aggressive." This labeling may be done by people who firmly believe in a traditional, stereotyped image for women. This image usually means that women are seen as grown-up girls. According to this belief system, to be feminine a woman should look pretty and be quiet. People holding this belief find assertive behavior unbecoming to a woman, so change can bring conflict. Be prepared for it.

Barbara's experience illustrates this quite well:

My relationship with Paul became very difficult. He really did not like the changes in me. He finally had to admit I was becoming more of an individual; I was no longer content just to be at home, no longer doing everything for him at home, no longer always available for him; and I was making my own demands on him to boot. I was taking time for myself and doing things that were important to me, more and more.

Things got so bad that we seriously considered separation. I was scared, but I couldn't go back to being the compassion-trap wife I used to be. Things are working out between us now, but that crisis showed me—and Paul—how strong I'd become. He never used any labels like "aggressive" on me, but I know it was hard for him to understand all the changes. At last, he's beginning to make some good changes of his own.

In learning to become more assertive you will need to remember the pendulum effect and the possibility of labeling by others. When you receive feedback from others that you have been aggressive, assess your words and actions by using the definitions for aggression and assertion in this chapter. You may decide the feedback is quite right. Thus it has helped you in your learning, and you can adjust your behavior accordingly. However, you may decide that the feedback is wrong or someone is mislabeling your behavior. Having considered the feedback and assessed it, you can keep it from having a negative effect on you by telling yourself your behavior was appropriately assertive. Thus you avoid being caught in the trap of allowing someone else to decide what is appropriate behavior for you and what your rights are. It is important during this learning process to be open to information and feedback from others. However, you also need to be able to use it wisely to continue learning and trying to change.

Becoming assertive may be very valuable to you. Most of all, you begin to experience more positive feelings about yourself and you feel more in control of your life. Even if you do not win in a situation, you are able to feel better because you handled it in a more competent, assertive manner. Each new situation that you feel you handle well is reinforcing and encouraging. It helps you to try other assertive behaviors and to accept your own rights.

As you begin to adopt a belief system that truly respects each individual's right to act assertively and to express honest thoughts, feelings, and beliefs, you may see others following your example. Earlier it was mentioned that your change will affect others in your life. As you are assertive, others may model your behavior.

Barbara's children quickly modeled her assertive behavior. She commented:

I noticed they were much better at expressing their feelings as I revealed my own emotions more honestly. And they were able to ask for what they wanted in shops and restaurants. Mark even asked for an overdone steak to be returned and replaced with a medium-rare one as he'd ordered.

I think the most significant effect of my assertiveness has been an improved relationship with my children. My being an assertive parent has benefited all of us.

Another major positive consequence is that you now have a choice about how you might act or react in a given situation. Part of that choice is *how* to respond assertively: honestly, directly, and appropriately, but with tact. Tactfulness is sometimes overlooked in being assertive, but it is an essential part of "appropriately." Lange and Jakubowski suggest four questions to ask yourself in determining *when* you should be assertive:[14]

1. How important is this situation to me?
2. How am I likely to feel afterwards if I don't assert myself in this situation?
3. How much will it cost me to assert myself in this situation?

4. Is it appropriate to assert myself in this situation?

If the answers to the questions are those that follow, then the choice will be to assert yourself.

1. very important
2. upset with myself; I'll mull over what I should have said for a day or so
3. might be uncomfortable, anxious for a short time
4. yes

On the other hand, if the answers are these, the choice will be to not assert yourself.

1. not important
2. probably will forget about it, feel fine
3. little cost, no anxiety
4. probably not, as the person would be extremely hurt

Hopefully, you are on your way to being able to communicate assertively, if that is your choice. Now that you have developed your assertiveness skills, you also have added to your communication skills. You have expanded your choices or alternatives in how to act and react in situations. It is your choice! To realize the self-fulfilling changes you are considering, it is important that you are able to communicate your needs, values, desires, and dreams to people who are important to you. Assertive communication is the most direct, constructive way to do this.

Assertiveness and a belief in your rights as a person are necessary for you to effect the changes in your life that you envision. It may take time, but the gradual, more consolidated changes are usually the long-standing, helpful ones.

LOOKING AT MY LIFE—38

- *My Learnings*

What have been the striking learnings for you out of this chapter? Some summary statements are included here to help you focus on your learning about assertive behavior.

I learned that I _____

I relearned that I _____

I became aware _____

I was surprised _____

I was pleased _____

I was disappointed _____

I see that I need to _____

I _____

I _____

SUGGESTED READING

Alberti, Robert E., & Emmons, Michael L. *Your perfect right* (Rev. ed.). San Luis Obispo, CA: Impact Press, 1974.

This book was written to help you overcome personal powerlessness. The authors feel that each person has the right to be and to express himself or herself and to feel good (not guilty) about doing so, as long as others are not hurt in the process. In reading this book you are urged to familiarize yourself with the concept of assertiveness and to apply the principles in your personal life.

Bloom, Lynn Z., Coburn, Karen, & Pearlman, Joan. *The new assertive woman.* New York: Delacorte Press, 1975.

Assertiveness is discussed on a personal level for women. The authors help you know what you feel and to say what you mean in many situations. The book is filled with dialogues, exercises, and personal success stories to help you learn to express yourself openly and appropriately.

Bower, Sharon A., & Bower, Gordon H. *Asserting yourself: a practical guide for positive change.* Menlo Park, CA: Addison-Wesley, 1976.

First, you learn how assertive you are now. Then the authors encourage you to follow a step-by-step program which helps improve your self-esteem, shows how to cope with stress, and how to look and feel assertive.

Jakubowski, Patricia, & Lange, Arthur J. *The assertive option: your rights and responsibilities.* Champaign, IL: Research Press, 1978.

This book presents a four-stage process to help you become more assertive by (1) identifying your personal rights and the rights of others, (2) discriminating between nonassertive, assertive, and aggressive behaviors, (3) identifying and changing the thoughts that are barriers to assertive behavior, and (4) practicing specific, new assertive behaviors. Several chapters focus on assertive behavior in specific situations, such as making and refusing requests, handling anger, carrying on conversations, and asserting yourself in intimate relationships.

Lange, Arthur J., & Jakubowski, Patricia. *Responsible assertive behavior: cognitive/behavioral procedures for trainers.* Champaign, IL: Research Press, 1976.

In the first chapters the authors present a rationale for assertion and discuss the causes of aggression and nonassertion. They also describe an assertive belief system, highlighting your personal rights as well as the rights of others. A series of structured exercises follow. Although primarily designed for trainers, the book is also useful for the individual and may help increase your awareness of criteria for an assertiveness training group.

Phelps, Stanlee, & Austin, Nancy. *The assertive woman.* San Luis Obispo, CA: Impact Press, 1975.

The authors are concerned with the feelings of anxiety, helplessness, and powerlessness that prevent a woman from choosing for herself, expressing her feelings, and having the confidence to ask for what she needs and wants. These areas are discussed with real-life examples followed by exercises to increase your awareness and assertiveness. Applications of the skills are well illustrated, and implications of acting assertively are discussed.

Nine

How Do I Put It All Together and Make It Work?

THE LAST FOUR STEPS

The purpose of this chapter is to help you bring together the information you have been collecting and considering in the other chapters. Then you can weigh this information in the light of your values and interests and hopefully make a well-considered decision leading directly to action. In this chapter you will be working through the last four steps in your decision-making process: evaluating the information on values and alternatives, choosing alternatives, taking action, and evaluating progress and reviewing the process.

Evaluating Values and Alternatives

First, it is important to review the information you have listed in previous chapters. In Chapter Three you made a list of values unique to you in relating to people. These values are important in determining a lifestyle that is fulfilling for you. Your experiences in education and in work (both paid and unpaid), your personal interests, hopes, and wishes were examined and clarified in Chapter Four. Later in Chapter Seven some typical alternatives were outlined.

•—•—•—•—•

LOOKING AT MY LIFE—39

- *My Alternatives*

Now you will be drawing this information together to list personal alternatives, which you will weigh in light of your situation and time management (Chapter Five) and in terms of the relative costs to you of changing (Chapter Six). The

LOOKING AT MY LIFE—39 (continued)

following chart will help you pull this information together and choose the best alternatives for you.

From the information you now have about yourself you can list the values, needs, wants, desires, and interests that are important to you in making your decision. These will be unique to you, coming from your analysis of yourself and your situation. Other women have listed such things as: time for myself, challenge, a salary, responsibility, security, a creative outlet, physical activity, independence, achievement, being with people, time for my husband, etc. As quickly as you can, list the things that are important to you in the left-hand column of the Alternatives Chart. They do not have to be in order of importance. You may want more time to consider your list, but write down what you can now; later you can add or subtract items.

Once you have completed this list, you are ready for the next part of the chart. Across the top, list the possible alternatives you are considering. These may be the ones you named in Chapter Seven, but include any new ideas that you have had along the way.

•━•━•━•

Women have used the chart to consider different types of alternatives. Some have weighed various alternatives to decide how to use their extra time, for example, working as a part-time volunteer at the hospital, as a full-time volunteer at the museum, or as a part-time aide in a library. Others have tried to decide on returning to school versus returning to work, for example, getting a university degree in accounting, working as a bank clerk, helping a husband with his books, or getting a community-college certificate in bookkeeping. For some women it has been a matter of deciding on various in-home activities, perhaps in combination with some outside ones; for example, pursuing a hobby or interest they have never had time for before; choices here might be weaving, painting, playing the piano, flying, getting back to a previous hobby, or becoming more physically active by joining a sports club. Still other women have weighed continuing their same activities against starting something new, like school or work.

ALTERNATIVES CHART

Alternatives to Consider

What I Value

These lists are offered as examples, not solutions, for you to consider. Each person's list of alternatives is tailor made out of her interests, wishes, and dreams.

Before considering the types of alternatives already suggested, you may feel it is necessary and important to deal with some alternatives which could be considered more basic: Is it better for me to remain in my marriage or to attempt a separation and/or divorce? If I remain in my marriage, what alternatives do I have to improve my relationship with my husband and children? Should I have a child or not? Will mother continue to live with me, or are there other approaches to her care that I should consider? Should I aim for that promotion? Is my husband going to change jobs and move our family across the country? Am I likely to keep living with my present mate? Should I get married?

Each of these more basic questions could profoundly affect your lifestyle and thus your choices. Perhaps you are a person who needs to look at one level of decisions before moving on to consider your options. Sometimes the specific basic question you need to consider has come to light after you have weighed information from the other chapters. If so, you will need to find the answers to this question before you continue with your original question.

If you find you have a series of questions rather than a single one, try to arrange them in a logical order. For example:

1. Is it better for me to remain in my marriage or to get a separation?
2. If I remain in the marriage, what alternatives do I have to improve it?
   — counseling as a couple?
   — parenting course?
   — communications course?
   — more commitment for me, leading to more happiness with myself?
3. If the marriage improves, what can I then do?
4. If I get a separation, what will I do to support myself, my children?

- need to return to school?
- work part time? full time?

Consider another decision with which you could be faced.

1. Will I (we) continue to live in this community or move to another place?
2. If I (we) remain here, what are my choices?
3. If I (we) move, how does that affect my options?
   - improve my range of choices or narrow it?
   - postpone my getting into anything different?
4. If the decision about moving is not immediate but in the offing, what can I do now that is transferable to a new community?

You can then approach each of these questions, using the type of chart that has been suggested. You may be able to approach these questions in this order, or you may find it helpful to explore answers to 2, 3, and 4 in both sets first to clarify the alternatives for Question 1 (both sets).

Choosing the Best Alternatives for You

LOOKING AT MY LIFE—40

- *Rank Order of my Alternatives*

Now you have focused on particular things that are important to you and the alternatives you wish to consider and evaluate. Using the information you charted, proceed to the next exercise which will help you consider and evaluate the alternatives, taking into consideration the list of things you value. Give weight to each alternative in light of these things you value. Use a weight from 1 to 5 to show how well this alternative meets your value, need, want, desire, or interest. The weightings indicate the following:

1. meets it not at all or slightly
2. meets it somewhat
3. meets it about 50-50
4. meets it quite well
5. meets it fully

LOOKING AT MY LIFE—40 (continued)

Take each alternative and weigh it against all your values and needs before moving on to the next alternative. This is sometimes difficult to do, so take your time and consider each idea carefully.

When you complete the chart, total the amounts for each alternative (Add each vertical column). This will give you a rank ordering of your alternatives based on your judgment of how well each meets the things that are important to you. If you total the points for each value (horizontal columns), as Barbara did, you will also be able to see which values are most important to you.

●━●━●━●

Were there any surprises for you? For some women the process of making the chart supports what they had thought, and they then feel more confident in choosing that alternative.

Others have been surprised at what emerges as the number one alternative. They may review the process again just to make sure they have done it correctly and have been honest with themselves. Sometimes this re-evaluation results in changes, but often the ranking remains the same. After reviewing it, though, a woman can more seriously consider the surprise alternative as the best for her.

As an example, you may be interested in how Barbara's chart looked (Figure 3, page 174). She had completed one chart while attending the Contemporary Woman Program. When she redid her values and alternatives recently, she was delighted to discover that she had accomplished most of the alternatives that she had considered four years earlier. Furthermore, she discovered that she was able to list many more values and some new alternatives on her new chart.

I have really learned a lot about myself and what I want to do. I now know I am more content pursuing activities that satisfy my needs. This process has really helped me be aware of myself as an individual, keep my goals clear, and review how much I've already done. This method sure keeps my priorities straight.

Taking Action

Now that you have rank ordered your alternatives, you are ready to plan how to put the first one into action. This is Step 5, and it is crucial. Planning the action will help you to ensure success as much as possible. Without clearly thinking through a plan of action, some women have immediately acted upon the alternative, only to meet failure and wonder why. Usually they conclude it was a wrong decision when it may really have been a good decision poorly put into action.

LOOKING AT MY LIFE—41

● *My Action Plan*

The following exercise is an action plan to help you consider both the hindrances and the helpful aspects you may face

Figure 3. Barbara's Alternatives Chart

Alternatives to Consider

What I Value		Contemporary Woman Leader	Consciousness-Raising Group	Travel Representative	Singing Group	Stampede Volunteer	Sports, Recreation	Travel	Math Upgrading	University, Social Work	SALT-Tourism Admin.	Reading	Retreat Home
		72	70	43	73	58	45	54	38	57	55	52	70
Independence	53	4	5	5	5	4	4	5	4	5	5	5	2
Intimacy	28	3	4	1	4	2	1	3	1	3	1	1	4
Communication	46	5	5	4	4	4	2	4	2	5	5	1	5
Health (Physical & Emotional)	47	5	5	1	5	2	5	4	2	4	4	5	5
Fun	47	4	4	4	5	5	5	5	1	2	2	5	5
Personal Growth	50	4	5	2	4	3	4	5	3	5	5	5	5
Mental Stimulation	54	5	5	3	4	4	3	5	5	5	5	5	5
Challenge	55	5	3	4	5	4	5	4	5	5	5	5	5
Recognition	41	5	5	3	5	4	1	1	3	5	5	1	3
Accomplishment	51	5	2	4	5	4	3	3	5	5	5	5	5
Interdependence	35	5	5	1	5	4	2	4	1	1	1	1	5
Involvement & People	48	5	5	3	5	5	4	4	1	5	5	1	5
Sense of Belonging	36	5	5	1	5	4	2	2	1	3	3	1	4
Need to be Needed	29	5	5	1	5	3	1	1	1	1	1	1	4
Sense of Uniqueness	35	4	5	3	5	4	1	2	1	1	1	4	4
Personal Financial Security	14	2	1	2	1	1	1	1	1	1	1	1	1
Privacy	18	1	1	1	1	1	1	1	1	1	1	5	3

LOOKING AT MY LIFE—41 (continued)

in putting your alternative into practice. You must realistically look ahead to the difficulties you are apt to meet and give some thought and preparation to overcoming them. Planning can help you feel confident to deal assertively with the problems that will arise. If you take time now to discover the positive, helpful aspects involved in putting the alternative into practice, you will have a solid boost before you begin. In completing the action plan, be as specific and concrete as you possibly can.

1. My goal is _____

_____

2. The specific concrete steps I will have to go through to reach my alternative or goal are:
   a. _____
   b. _____
   c. _____
   d. _____
   e. _____

3. How strongly committed am I to making this change (Place an X in the appropriate space)?

Not committed   Very committed

4. What are the forces within me, in my relationships, or in my environment that may hinder me from reaching my goal?
   a. Hindering forces within *myself*
      (for example, personal characteristics, values, or skills: patience, laziness, disorganization, lack of confidence, aggressiveness, passiveness, inability to drive):

   _____

   _____

   _____

   _____

LOOKING AT MY LIFE—41 (continued)

How can I work with or around these forces?

_____

_____

_____

_____

b.   Hindering forces in my *relationships*
(for example, family disapproval, lack of financial
help, disapproval from friends):

_____

_____

_____

_____

How can I work with or around these forces?

_____

_____

_____

_____

c.   Hindering forces in my *environment*
(for example, class I want is not offered):

_____

_____

_____

_____

How can I work with or around these forces?

_____

_____

_____

_____

5. What are the forces within me, in my relationships, or in
my environment that may help me reach my alternative or
goal?

a. Helpful forces within *myself*
(for example, personal characteristics, values, or skills: patience, perserverance, cheerfulness, organization, versatility, assertiveness, typing skills):

_____

_____

_____

_____

How will I use these forces?

_____

_____

_____

_____

b. Helpful forces in my *relationships*
(for example, moral and financial support from my husband or mate, support from my children, encouragement from my friends):

_____

_____

_____

_____

How will I use these forces?

_____

_____

_____

_____

c. Helpful forces in my *environment*
(for example, excellent volunteer bureau, a university only 10 miles away, the possibility of having two people do one job):

_____

_____

_____

_____

LOOKING AT MY LIFE—41 (continued)

How will I use these forces?

_____
_____
_____
_____

6. How will I communicate to my family and my friends my alternative or goal and how much it means to me?

_____
_____
_____
_____

7. Who outside of the situation or relationship I am trying to change would I like to help and support me in putting into action my change process leading to my alternative or goal?

_____
_____
_____
_____

In what ways do I feel this person would be effective in helping me?

_____
_____
_____
_____

8. How will I know when I am making progress toward my alternative or goal?

_____
_____
_____
_____

How will I know when I have reached my alternative or goal?

_____

_____

_____

_____

9. When in the future will I review my progress in reaching my alternative or goal?

_____

_____

_____

_____

•➖•➖•➖•

The action plan you have outlined can now be your springboard. You are ready to go—excited, confident, and yet a little scared. There will undoubtedly be a mix of feelings. You are beginning something you really want to do, which makes you excited and eager. It is different from what you have been doing. It can involve some risk, which accounts for some of that excitement but also some fear. That is realistic. Usually the excitement and eagerness will help push you on your way. If by chance you feel the fear starting to overwhelm you, reread your alternatives chart and the chapter on assertiveness to buck up your courage.

You are ready. Great! Before you start, read farther to ensure that you do not overlook the very last step in the decision-making process: evaluating progress and reviewing the process.

•➖•➖•➖•

Evaluating Progress and Reviewing the Process

The last two steps of the action plan you have already made involve important aspects of the decision-making process: evaluating progress and reviewing the process. You listed ways you will know when you have reached your alternative. This list gives you criteria for progress so that you can judge how well you are doing. What most often seems to happen is that a woman has gone through five steps toward her goal, but she feels like she is making no progress. By having the criteria clearly outlined you will be better able to evaluate your progress and to say reinforcing things to yourself as a reward. Keeping your progress clearly in mind will inspire you to continue.

Setting a specific time when you will review your progress is also useful. You can evaluate progress and review the process. This review will not only help you to know how well you are doing but also will encourage you to think of new ideas that can help you move toward your alternative faster. By review time you probably will have new information about hindrances and helpful aspects. By periodically reviewing your progress and the process, you will be able to continue to put new information into your action plan. Thus the action plan becomes a dynamic helping force rather than just a list. This incorporation of new information may also involve going back to some of the earlier steps in the decision-making process. Remember, the process, too, is dynamic. It is flexible and open to new information. Two examples may better explain these ideas.

Trudy discovered that a family friend wished to offer her a full-time position as a receptionist and bookkeeper—exactly what she wanted to do. However, she had originally decided to work part time. This new possibility sent Trudy back to her alternatives chart to add the new one and to reconsider her choices. She decided she would still like to work part time because of the high value she placed on spending time at home with her family. Another consideration was her feeling that a full-time position would cause undue pressure and thus detract from her goals of independence and satisfaction. Having carefully reviewed this alternative in light of her needs and values, Trudy approached the family friend with confidence in her decision. She indicated that while she appreciated the offer, she would only be able to accept it on a part-time basis. The prospective employer admired her forthrightness but still wanted a full-time worker. However, he knew a company which had the type of position Trudy wanted and referred her to them.

Another example of re-entering the decision-making process, although at an earlier stage, is the following. Betty had decided to return to school on a part-time basis, and gradually over a period of 7 years, she would finish a university degree in chemistry. One at a time, she had taken 5 courses, had found them stimulating and enjoyable, and had received grades ranging from C+ to A. One day she returned from class to find her husband packing a suitcase. He told her he had decided to leave her and the children. His lawyer would be contacting her about divorce proceedings. Her husband's sudden departure was a great shock to Betty. Her financial situation seemed precarious. She was not sure if she would need to get a job immediately. She had no training other than her five university courses. Also, because of the emotional upheaval she was experiencing, she questioned her values and needs. At a time such as this, when critical and drastic emotional upheaval is occurring, it is often helpful to discuss concerns with a close friend or a counselor who can help you to be more objective.

It was important for Betty to return to Step 2 in the decision-making process to review her personal traits as an emotional booster and to review her values. This second look helped her regain some of her confidence in her own abilities. Then she reviewed her alternatives chart, adding the new alternative of immediately going to work, the new values of emotional independence, and the security of a steady income. She omitted time with her husband but remembered to replace it with time for good friends. She recognized the need for emotional support during this transition period. Having reconsidered her alternatives, Betty suggested to her lawyer that she approach her husband for financial help to complete her chemistry training. This would be an investment for him since she would be better able to find a position that would pay enough to help support herself and the children. She was prepared to take more courses and to apply the chemistry credits she had already taken to a shorter community college program in environmental control. She did not want to attend full time since she now had total responsibility for their three children. This solution was acceptable to her husband and became part of the divorce settlement.

Looking back on the process, Betty also realized a constructive side benefit. Studying and working toward her goal helped her regain her confidence and gave her the satisfaction of knowing she was working to build a sound future.

When Barbara looked back on the long process she went through to provide some direction to her life, she realized how time consuming and difficult it had been.

When I began examining my own situation, I didn't think it would take as long as it has. I said to myself I'll just get my life together and go from there! It doesn't work that way. It's long, tedious, and really hard. I found it really hard to look inside, but it gets easier after a while, too. And then it became a real challenge for me. Something important for me has been having long-range goals. But I also try to live daily—maybe have many goals including some immediate goals and some long-range ones. And I try to be flexible. I think being rigid in getting something would be a really bad thing for me.

I had to realize that things don't happen overnight and that change is constant. I am changing and maybe what I am saying to you today will also change. Three years from now or five years from now I may be doing quite different things from what I now expect to be doing. There are so many things that could happen between now and then. Maybe I will get into something and decide I don't like it. But that's OK now. I didn't know that was OK back a few years ago. It was like having blinders on.

That's why flexibility is so important. It's all tied up with becoming more aware of many things, too. And part of the problem is knowing there are so many routes to go. There are so many choices, and sometimes making choices isn't easy!!

It's been good for me, really good, just exploring things. It makes me a better person, too—or one I like better.

Many women struggle through the process in a way similar to Barbara's description. As usual, there are great individual differences: Some women breeze through the process, others struggle painfully through each small step, and others fall somewhere in the middle. At times you may move along quickly, but there will probably also be some slow, struggling times. Hopefully, the examples of Barbara and other women in this book will help encourage you. Sometimes it may seem to you that Barbara is Wonder Woman II. That is not true! She is a fairly typical woman of today. Looking back on her life, she is able to describe the situation and her feelings very well. However, there have been times she felt lost, confused, and uncertain. She has learned that some of those feelings may be a necessary accompaniment to change and growth. Most of the time the process of decision making is important, necessary, and even enjoyable. Also do remember that as you progress toward your goal, you may encounter new information that causes you to alter your goal. That often makes the process more enjoyable and certainly makes life interesting and vital.

THE GOAL

To be a person you like better—that's our goal for the people who have read this book, struggled with the exercises, and worked through to an action plan. Congratulations! It has been a long process, and it will go on. Hopefully, it has been a rewarding and enriching experience. You now have skills to cope with future decisions. We hope, too, that you have the conviction to act on your decisions and in doing so, confidence that you are following through on the best decision available to you. We hope we have helped you make a change but left you free to decide what and how to change.

To close, we include an anonymous poem which women in our groups have found moving and encouraging. Good luck on your personal decision making, risk taking, and living life to the fullest.

A TIME TO RISK

To laugh is to risk appearing the fool.
  To weep is to risk appearing sentimental.
    To reach out for another is to risk involvement.

To expose feelings is to risk exposing your true self.
  To place your ideas, your dreams before the crowd is to
    risk loss.
    To love is to risk not being loved in return.

To live is to risk dying.
  To hope is to risk despair.
    To try at all is to risk failure.

        But risk we must.

Because the greatest hazard to life is to risk nothing.
  The woman who risks nothing
                    does nothing
                      has nothing
                        is nothing.

She may avoid suffering . . . but
  She simply cannot learn, feel, change, grow, love, live.

Chained by her certitudes, she is a slave; she has forfeited
  freedom.
  Only the person who risks can be called a free person.

                                        Anonymous

SUGGESTED READING

Krantzler, Mel. *Creative divorce.* New York: Signet Books, 1974.

Krantzler deals with the feelings of men and women who face the need to build new lives in the wake of loneliness, guilt, anger, rejection, and a sense of failure. The book offers a positive program for accepting your divorce as a solution, not a punishment; for laying your past to rest; and for reaching out toward new, healthier relationships.

Miller, Sherod; Nunnally, Elam W.; & Wackman, Daniel B. *Alive and aware: improving communication in relationships.* Minneapolis, MN: Interpersonal Communications Programs, 1975.

The goals of this book are to increase your awareness of how you communicate and to increase specific skills that will help you communicate more effectively and flexibly. The emphasis is on development rather than problems.

Rogers, Carl. *Becoming partners: marriage and its alternatives.* New York: Dell, 1972.

Using interviews and the individual's own words, Rogers describes a series of relationships, breakdowns, and restructurings in a wide variety of partnerships. These are followed by commentary and summation. Various alternatives are presented but are not judged as being good or bad.

Yates, Martha. *Coping: a survival manual for women alone.* Englewood Cliffs, NJ: Prentice-Hall, 1976.

There are more than 15 million single, widowed, or divorced women in the U.S.A. These women hold jobs, maintain homes, pay bills, raise children, and live as single women in a couple-oriented society. If you are in one of these categories, this book will help you meet these and other responsibilities with practical, down-to-earth ideas on handling money, insurance, income tax, and credit; guiding your children through a readjustment period following your widowhood or divorce; and coping with your own emotions and doubts so you can become a more vital person.

Epilogue

It is our hope that this book has helped you in the process of making a decision that will affect your lifestyle in a constructive manner. Hopefully, in following the decision-making steps you have been able:

— to be honest with yourself.
— to feel more confident and act more assertively.
— to be realistic.
— to develop a constructive support system with your family and friends.
— to take more risks.

Most of all, we hope you feel happier and more pleased with yourself. We think these are rewards that are built into the system suggested here.

One aspect of writing this book that has been especially difficult for us is the inability to have two-way communication with you. In working with women individually and in groups, we have always been able to obtain reactions about how well our suggestions fit for each unique woman. We attempt to apply the model of using new information and feedback to ourselves and what we do. Thus reactions from women in our groups, and also from you, provide vital new information for us to consider in continuing our work.

We have outlined the general procedures and steps which appear to apply universally. Care must be taken to tailor the approach to fit you. We would appreciate hearing how the book has helped you. What parts seemed to apply and fit you best? What parts were difficult? What parts did not apply or were not helpful? What did you decide to do? How has it affected your life? Your family? Others close to you? It is helpful to us to receive both the positive and the negative feedback. We look forward to hearing from you about your experiences. Please write to us at:

Student Counselling Services
University of Calgary
Calgary, Alberta
Canada   T2N 1N4

Notes

Chapter 1

    1. *Monthly vital statistics report.* Washington, D.C.: U.S. Department of Health, Education, and Welfare, Public Health Services, Health Resources Administration, October 24, 1974.

Chapter 3

    1. J. Eason. Life-style counseling for a reluctant leisure class. *Personnel and Guidance Journal,* 1972, *51* (2), 127-132.

    2. L. G. Hall & R. B. Tarrier. *Hall occupational orientation inventory manual* (3rd ed.). Bensenville, IL: Scholastic Testing Services, 1976; A. L. Edwards. *Edwards personal preference schedule manual.* New York: Psychological Corporation, 1959; A. H. Maslow. *Motivation and personality.* New York: Harper & Brothers, 1954; H. A. Murray et al. *Explorations in personality.* New York: Oxford University Press, 1938.

    3. Hall & Tarrier, 1976.

    4. Who's News. *New Woman Magazine,* June, 1977, 25.

Chapter 4

    1. E. E. Matthews, S. N. Feingold, B. Weary, J. Berry, & L. E. Tyler. *Counseling girls and women over the life span.* Washington, D.C.: National Vocational Guidance Association, 1972.

    2. J. I. Holland. *Making vocational choices: a theory of careers.* Englewood Cliffs, NJ: Prentice-Hall, Inc., 1973.

Chapter 6

    1. L. W. Hoffman & F. I. Nye. *Working mothers: an evaluative review of the consequences for wife, husband, and child.* San Francisco: Jossey-Bass, 1974.

2. M. Adams. The compassion trap. In V. Gornick & B. Moran (Eds.), *Woman in a sexist society: studies in power and powerlessness.* New York: Basic Books, Inc., 1971, p. 556.

3. Adams, 1971, p. 559.

4. R. Stuart. Lecture. Institute of Psychiatry, London, England, January, 1976.

5. J. Bernard. *The future of marriage.* New York: Macmillan, 1971; J. Bernard. The paradox of a happy marriage. In V. Gornick & B. Moran (Eds.), *Woman in a sexist society: studies in power and powerlessness.* New York: Basic Books, Inc., 1971; J. Bernard. *Women, wives, mothers: values and options.* Chicago: Aldine Publishing Co., 1975.

6. Hoffman & Nye, 1974.

7. Hoffman & Nye, 1974.

Chapter 7

1. *1969 handbook on women workers.* Women's Bureau Bulletin. Washington, D.C.: U.S. Department of Labor, Wage and Labor Standards Administration, 1969.

2. E. Lenz & M. H. Shaevitz. *So you want to go back to school: facing the realities of re-entry.* New York: McGraw-Hill, 1977.

3. *Flexible work schedules: a Catalyst position paper.* New York: Catalyst, 1973; *Profiles of individuals in paired positions.* New York: Catalyst, 1973.

4. M. M. Ferree. The confused American housewife. *Psychology Today,* September, 1976, 76-80; A. Oakley. *The sociology of housework.* London: Martin Robertson, 1974.

Chapter 8

1. V. C. Plenge. The effects of assertive training and group counselling on assertiveness and self-esteem in middle class women. Unpublished master's thesis, University of Calgary, 1976. (Microfilm)

2. R. E. Alberti & M. L. Emmons. *Your perfect right* (Rev. ed.). San Luis Obispo, CA: Impact Press, 1974.

3. P. Jakubowski. Assertive behavior and clinical problems of women. In E. I. Rawlings & D. K. Carter (Eds.), *Psycho-*

therapy for women: treatment toward equality. Springfield, IL: Charles C. Thomas, 1977, p. 147.

4. A. J. Lange & P. Jakubowski. *Responsible assertive behavior: cognitive/behavioral procedures for trainers.* Champaign, IL: Research Press, 1976.

5. Jakubowski, 1977, p. 147.

6. Lange & Jakubowski, 1976, p. 10.

7. G. R. Bach & P. Wyden. *The intimate enemy.* New York: Avon Books, 1968.

8. S. A. Bower & G. H. Bower. *Asserting yourself: a practical guide for positive change.* Menlo Park, CA: Addison-Wesley, 1976.

9. Bower & Bower, 1976, p. 90.

10. A. Ellis & R. A. Harper. *A new guide to rational living.* Englewood Cliffs, NJ: Prentice-Hall, 1975.

11. P. Jakubowski & A. J. Lange. *The assertive option: your rights and responsibilities.* Champaign, IL: Research Press, 1978.

12. Lange & Jakubowski, 1976, p. 55.

13. Lange & Jakubowski, 1976, p. 56.

14. Lange & Jakubowski, 1976, p. 64.

About the Authors

Lorna Cammaert and Carolyn Larsen are psychologists who have worked together for 10 years developing many counseling programs for women. These have included the Contemporary Woman Programs, assertiveness training, career and female sexuality workshops, and conferences and seminars for professionals involved in counseling girls and women. They have developed television programs, carried out research on women, and presented papers at professional meetings.

Dr. Cammaert received her Ph.D. in counseling psychology from the University of Oregon in 1968. She currently holds a joint appointment as a counselor at the Student Counselling Services and as an associate professor in the Department of

Educational Psychology, The University of Calgary. She has developed a graduate course in counseling girls and women. She was a single career woman until her marriage 5 years ago and currently combines her roles as psychologist, wife, and part-time mother of three children from her husband's first marriage.

Dr. Larsen received a Ph.D. in clinical psychology from Indiana University in 1963. She worked for 3 years in Connecticut as a therapist in a child guidance clinic and then taught for several years in the Psychology and Psychiatry Departments at the University of Alberta. She is currently a counselor at the Student Counselling Services, The University of Calgary. For over 18 years she has combined the roles of wife and mother with a part-time, then a full-time, career.